CP/M

Revealed

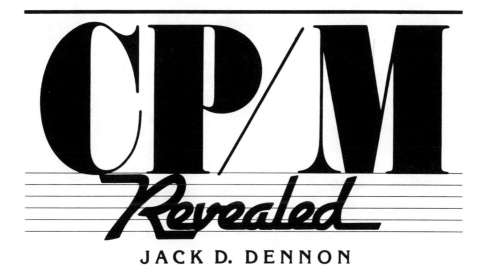

CP/M Revealed

JACK D. DENNON

HAYDEN BOOK COMPANY, INC.
Rochelle Park, New Jersey

Library of Congress Cataloging in Publication Data

Dennon, Jack D.
  CP/M revealed.

  Includes index.
  1. CP/M (Computer program)   I. Title.   II. Title:
C.P./M. revealed.
QA76.6.D46 1982   001.64'25   82-15589
ISBN   0-8104-5204-9

Printed in the United States of America

1	2	3	4	5	6	7	8	9	PRINTING
82	83	84	85	86	87	88	89	90	YEAR

Preface

WE SET OUT in this book on the assumption that the reader may have no prior computer experience but does have access to an "up and running" CP/M system.

The reader should have access to a CP/M system that includes the Digital Research text editor, assembler, and debug utilities. These utilities, provided by Digital Research with each CP/M system, are the basic tools available in CP/M for the exploration of CP/M. The first chapter includes introductory programming exercises using Microsoft BASIC and Compiler Systems CBASIC. If either of these is not available, the exercise may be omitted.

All of the remaining exercises require only the basic CP/M utilities. The assembler is the primary programming tool used. The reader will learn to use assembly code without having to fully understand assembly language programming. Each exercise is worked out in detail and should be performed by the reader at the computer console keyboard. The exercises provide progressive lessons using CP/M to explore CP/M.

Chapters 1 through 4 are an introduction to the computer and provide sufficient background to bring with reach the Digital Research CP/M manuals and their coverage of visible CP/M features. Remaining chapters explore the less visible features, characteristics, and properties of CP/M.

A primary goal of this book is to explore both the visible and the invisible portions of CP/M. For so long as misunderstandings do not arise, invisibility is a desirable feature relating to the elegance with which CP/M makes complex operations appear effortless. But invisibility combined with misunderstanding brings progress to a halt. The CP/M insights provided by the exercises in this book reduce significantly the incidence of misunderstanding.

To expedite the exercises, the reader should have available, in addition to the Digital Research CP/M manuals, an Intel 8080/8085 machine instruction reference guide, the computer start-up and shut-down instructions, and disk loading and unloading instructions provided with the computer. All 8080 instructions, of course, do execute on Z80, and Z80 users can gain the most from this book by referring to both the 8080/8085 and Z80 reference manuals.

Contents

CHAPTER 1

Introduction to CP/M

*L*ET'S ASSUME THAT you are at the console keyboard of a CP/M system that is up and running (in other words, the computer has been powered up and the CP/M loaded into it). We will assume that this CP/M system includes a console with a typewriter-like keyboard, a video display screen, one or more disks, and a printer.

The System Prompt

First you press the keyboard *space bar*. Something on the screen should move; that something is called the *cursor*. The cursor may be a small rectangle, an underline, an overline, or the like. When you press the space bar, CP/M "reads," or takes in, the character from the keyboard, stores it, and "echos" it back to the screen—that is, displays it once again. To the computer, the blank created by the space bar is a *character*, just as any letter—A, B, C, etc.—is a character.

Now press the key for the letter A. If the computer echos a capital letter A, shift your keyboard to lower-case, if possible, and press the A key again. Then press the key marked *Return* or *Enter*. Whether you have entered Aa or aa, the computer should respond with

  AA?

The Console Command Processor

The CP/M Console Command Processor, called *CCP*, always "folds" (that is, converts), to upper-case all characters it receives from the keyboard. This is a property of CCP only, not of CP/M generally. CCP is used mainly for getting other programs started. Once another program has been started, case folding may or may not occur; it depends on the program.

Each time you press the Enter or Return key, the CCP will redisplay its *prompt*. The prompt is a letter, usually A, followed by an arrowhead-shaped symbol, as follows:

$$A >$$

This prompt means that CCP is waiting for your next *command*.

Command Entry

If you type in the letters ABCDE or abcde and then press the key marked *Delete* or *Rubout*, some CP/M systems will move the cursor back over the line and erase it, removing one character every time the key is pressed. Other systems will echo each character as it is removed or deleted. In either case, you can redisplay the entire text line as it is currently stored by holding down the *Control* or *CTRL* key and simultaneously pressing the letter R key, called *Control-R*.

Any time before pressing Enter or Return, you can cancel the entire current line being typed by holding down Control and simultaneously pressing the letter X key, called *Control-X*.

If you make a mistake typing, use Rubout or Delete to backspace or Control-X to start over. If at any time you get confused as to what you've actually typed in, use Control-R to make CP/M redisplay the entire line as currently stored in its line buffer.

An Exercise Using Microsoft BASIC

A good program for an introduction to computing is Microsoft BASIC. The first thing you need to do is find out if this BASIC is available to your system. To do so, simply "call" it and see what happens. Using either upper- or lower-case, type

BASIC

and then press the Enter or Return key.

If BASIC is not available, CCP will respond by repeating the command we entered with a question mark, as follows:

BASIC?

This response means that CCP did not find BASIC in the directory of the disk we are using. (*Note:* Microsoft BASIC may be available under a different name. This exercise is the only place in this book that we refer to Microsoft BASIC. Neither this exercise nor the succeeding one that uses CBASIC is required for understanding the material that follows.)

If BASIC is available, however, CCP will load it into the computer, display several lines of information on the screen, and then wait for you to type something in. Assuming that BASIC has been found, type in this line, followed by Enter or Return:

> *100   input "What is your name" ; n$*

Then type in the following line, again followed by Enter or Return:

> *200   print "Hi " ; n$; "!"*

Now type the command,

> *list*

followed by Enter or Return. In response, you should get these three lines displayed on the screen:

> *100   INPUT "What is your name" ; N$*
> *200   PRINT "Hi " ; N$; "!"*
> *OK*

The first two lines of your program are called a *listing*. The line OK is called a *prompt*. If there are any errors, correct them by typing the entire line over again. BASIC will delete the old line for you.

To execute your program, type the command

> *run*

followed by Enter or Return. Your program will respond with the line

> *What is your name?*

Answer by typing your name, for example,

> *Jeani*

followed by Enter or Return. Your program will respond with

> *Hi Jeani!*

Modifying the Program

Having made friends with the computer, you are ready for more advanced exercises. You can modify your program by adding the following two lines:

> *50   def usr1 = 0*
> *75   x = usr1(x)*

following each line with Enter or Return. List your program and examine it carefully to be sure you're using the number zero and not the letter "oh" in line 50. Correct any errors by typing the entire line over again, and the old line will be automatically deleted. Run your modified program by typing the command Run followed by Enter or Return.

Your modified program will simply "jump" to a location in memory that takes you out of BASIC and brings you back to CCP. Later, you may want to explore BASIC in more detail, but since our primary goal is to learn about CP/M, we are going to move on to discuss the CP/M text editor, called *ED*.

The CP/M Text Editor

The CP/M text editor is used to create and modify *text files*. For it to do so, you first have to decide upon a name for each file. Each name has to be unique. Therefore, before you can select a particular name, you have to know all those names already in use.

Selecting a File Name
The CCP directory display command,

> *DIR*

will display all file names currently being used. A more selective way to discover if a particular name, say HELLO.BAS, is available (that is, not already being used) is to change the form of the directory command to

> *DIR HELLO.BAS*

followed by Enter or Return. If the name HELLO.BAS is available, the CCP will respond with

> *NOT FOUND*

or

> *NO FILE*

If a file named HELLO.BAS already exists, then try names such as MYHELLO.BAS, NEWHELLO.BAS, HITHERE.BAS, or the like, until you find a name that is available. Any name of up to eight letters may be used, but it must always be followed by .BAS. If your selected name is not HELLO, then throughout the following exercise use your own file name wherever HELLO appears.

Using the Editor
The CP/M text editor can be called with the CCP command,

> *ED HELLO.BAS*

followed by Enter or Return. CCP will load and start the editor, and then the editor will display the message,

> *NEW FILE*

followed by an asterisk (*) to indicate that it is ready for a command.

Type in a lower-case letter i followed by Enter or Return. The editor will advance the display to a new line but otherwise will give no response. This command places the editor in *insert-mode*, sometimes also called *input-mode*.

Now type in these two lines,

> *input "What is your name?" ; n$*
> *print "Hi " ; n$; "!"*

following each line with Enter or Return, and then enter a Control-Z by holding down the key marked Control and simultaneously pressing the letter Z. The editor will respond with an asterisk (*) to show that it has exited the input-mode and is back in *command-mode*.

If you want to review what you've typed in, type the command B followed by Enter or Return. This command moves the text pointer back to the beginning of the text buffer. If you then type the command #T followed by Enter or Return, the editor will type out the contents of the text buffer, which should consist of everything you typed in during input-mode. The editor, in short, is in input-mode from the command i until the command Control-Z.

Correcting Typing Errors with the Substitute Command
To illustrate text correction with the editor, suppose that your first line reads

> *input "What os your name?" ; n$*

The typing error "os" can be quickly corrected, and the correction verified, by the command

> *sos↑Zis↑Z0lt*

where "sos" means "substitute for os"; ↑Z is a symbol for Control-Z, entered by holding Control and pressing Z just as we did earlier; and 0lt means "put the character pointer at the beginning of the current line and then type the current line out." (Notice that 0lt represents "zero-el-tee," not "oh-el-tee.")

You can always use Control-R to review any command line before executing it.

For a complete description of this and other editor commands, you will want to study the Digital Research editor manual, "ED: A Context Editor for the CP/M Disk System."

Ending the Edit Session
When you are finished making corrections, you can conclude the editing session by typing E or e followed by Enter or Return. This editor command is called, simply enough, the *end command*.

Compiling and Running a Program

To compile the program that you have created in the file named HELLO.BAS, you will want to determine if CBASIC is available. To do so, use the directory command,

> *DIR CBAS2.COM*

If CBASIC is available, CCP will respond with the following:

> *A: CBAS2 COM*

CBASIC may be available under a different name. You can create a display of all available command files with the CCP command,

> *DIR *.COM*

If CBASIC is available under a name other than CBAS2, then use that other name in this exercise wherever CBAS2 appears.

Let's assume that CBASIC is available. The command to call the CBASIC compiler and have it compile your program is

> *CBAS2 HELLO*

The compiler will list your program on the screen as it is compiled and then display a few lines of information about it, at which time CCP will regain control. If the compiler indicates

> *NO ERRORS DETECTED*

then you can run your program by calling the CBASIC run time monitor, called *CRUN2*. If CRUN2 is available under another name, then use that other name in this exercise wherever CRUN2 appears.

To run your program, type the command

> *CRUN2 HELLO*

followed by Enter or Return. Your program will then ask

> *What is your name?*

Answer by typing in your name, for example,

> *Jeani*

followed by Enter or Return. Your program will respond with

> *Hi Jeani!*

and then control will return to CCP.

Modifying the Program with the Editor

You can now use the editor to modify your program. Begin, as before, with the command

> *ED HELLO.BAS*

This time, the editor doesn't respond with NEW FILE but only with an asterick(*) because the file HELLO.BAS already exists.

To tell the editor to bring the entire file into its text buffer, use the command #A followed by Enter or Return. (Since # literally means 65535, #A means "append 65535 lines, or as many lines as the buffer will hold, whichever occurs first.) The editor will respond with another asterisk (*) when it is prepared for your next command.

To obtain the first line in the text buffer, type the letter T followed by Enter or Return. The line displayed should be the first line of your program,

input "What is your name?" ; n$

To prefix a statement number to this line, use the command

i100↑Z0lt

followed by Enter or Return. Remember to use "zero-el-tee," not "oh-el-tee," and also remember that the symbol ↑Z represents Control -Z.

To display the second line of the program, type Enter or Return. To insert a new line of text in front of the displayed line, first type i followed by Enter or Return in order to enter insert-mode, and then type the new text:

if n$ = "Jack" then go to 200

followed by Enter or Return. Now get out of insert-mode with Control-Z.

Position the text pointer to the end of the text buffer by typing –B followed by Enter or Return. Go back to insert-mode with i followed by Enter or Return, and type these two new lines of text at the end of the program:

go to 100
200   print "What are you doing here?"

following each line with Enter or Return. Type Control-Z to exit input-mode and use the B command to put the text pointer back to the beginning of the text buffer.

By now you should be so tired of being reminded to follow each command and text line with Enter or Return that you will remember to do so without any prompting.

Listing a Modified Program

To list your modified program, use the #T command. Your program should then look like this:

100   input "What is your name?" ; n$
if n$ = "Jack" then go to 200
print "Hi " ; n$; "!"
go to 100
200   print "What are you doing here!"

If your program is displayed correctly, end the edit session with the E command.

Compiling a Modified Program

When CCP responds with its prompt, you can compile your modified program with the command

CBAS2 HELLO

If the compiler indicates any errors in the source code, you will have to correct the source code file HELLO.BAS. If your computer system includes a printer, you can create a hardcopy listing of the source file by using the Peripheral Interchange Program, called *PIP*, to print out the file HELLO.BAS on the printer. To do so, use the command

PIP LST:=HELLO.BAS

If no printer is available, you can display the listing on the screen with the command

TYPE HELLO.BAS

Compare your listing with the program shown in Fig. 1.1. If the error is not apparent, it may be helpful to have CBASIC itself create a listing that will include any error messages. To do so, first put CP/M into console-print mode by holding down the Control key and simultaneously pressing the letter P, called *Control-P*. Then call the compiler again with the command

CBAS2 HELLO

After the compilation is complete, exit from console-print mode by entering another Control-P.

The text editor can be used as it was earlier to correct the text file HELLO.BAS. To recompile, use the command

CBAS2 HELLO

When the compiler responds

NO ERRORS DETECTED

you can run your new program with the command

CRUN2 HELLO

Your new program will say hello to almost everyone.

```
100 input "What is your name?" ; n$
if n$="Jack" then go to 200
print "Hi ";n$;"!"
go to 100
200 print "What are you doing here!"
```

Fig. 1.1 *CBASIC version of HELLO*

Summary

In this CP/M session you have become acquainted with two versions of the powerful and popular BASIC programming language. You have used the CP/M text editor to create and modify a computer program; you have been introduced to a compiler and to the idea of a file name; and you have begun to develop some idea of what it is like to work with a computer through CP/M.

You will have gained valuable experience from this chapter if you've actually worked the exercises. In the chapters that follow, especially if you are a beginner at computing, it is imperative that you actually do the exercises. The capsule summary at the end of each chapter cannot compensate for the know-how lost if the exercises are skipped. In the absence of "hands-on" experience, the barrier to communication will become virtually impenetrable.

CHAPTER 2

The CP/M Text Editor

*I*N THE FIRST chapter you were introduced to the CP/M text editor. In this chapter, the editor will be discussed in more general terms.

File Names

The CP/M text editor can be called only by a CCP command of the form

>   *ED ufn*

where ufn is an *unambiguous file name*, that is, a file name containing neither a question mark (?) nor an asterisk (*).

The CCP directory command, in contrast, will accept an *ambiguous file name*, or afn, in commands such as

>   *DIR *.BAS*

and

>   *DIR HELLO?.COM*

During a CP/M directory search, the asterisk of the first command above matches any file name, and the question mark of the second matches any character.

Finding and Creating a Named File

The editor will either find a named file or create it. If the editor finds the named file, then it will display an asterisk (*) to show that it is in command-mode.

If it doesn't find the named file, then it will create a file directory entry for that name and display the message

> *NEW FILE*

on the screen to show that it has created a new directory entry.

Creating New Text or Appending Old Text

New text can be created by putting the editor into insert-mode with the i command. If the needed file exists, old text can be brought into the text buffer in memory with the a, or *append, command.*

The size of the editor's text buffer depends on the size of your computer's main memory. In a minimum memory system, the editor's buffer will hold about 6000 characters. In a maximum memory system, the buffer will hold somewhat more than 40,000 characters.

An Exercise

Let's go through part of an exercise described in the Digital Research ED manual. First, use the command

> *DIR *.TMP*

to verify that "TEST.TMP" does not already exist. Then call the editor with the command

> *ED TEST.TMP*

The editor should respond

> *NEW FILE*

and then display the command-mode prompt (*).

Now put the editor into upper-case insert-mode with the I command. Type the three lines

> *Now is the*
> *time for*
> *all good men*

and follow each line with Enter or Return. (The Enter or Return key—also called *carriage return*—is denoted in the ED manual by *cr*.) Get out of insert-mode with Control-Z.

Try a type command by typing T followed by carriage return. Nothing will be typed out, thereby confirming that the text pointer, or character pointer, is positioned at the end of the text, as illustrated at the top of page 6 of the ED manual.

The command B2T will move the pointer to the beginning of the text and then type out two lines. The pointer remains at the beginning of the text.

The command 5C0T will move the pointer forward five character positions and then display text from the beginning of the current line up to the position of the pointer. The result is

NOW I

We find that the characters in the text buffer are all upper-case. Case folding occurred because we used an I command to put the editor into insert-mode. If we had used an i command, the characters would not have folded to upper-case. In other words, an i command will put exactly what you type into the text buffer. Case folding is invoked implicitly when a command letter is typed in upper-case. For example, the *find command* Fthis will search for "THIS" rather than "this."

The command 2L−T will move the character pointer forward two lines and then type the line preceding the character pointer. The result is

TIME FOR

The command −L#K will move the character pointer back one line and then delete all lines following the pointer. We are left with one line in the text buffer and the pointer positioned at the end of that line.

A Sufficient Set of Editing Tools

A subset of editor commands that will provide sufficient tools for succeeding exercises is as follows:

a	*append*	To bring in old text
i	*insert*	To create new text
t	*type*	To type out text lines
s	*sub*	To substitute new text for old
f	*find*	To find strings in the current buffer
n	*next*	To find strings anywhere in the file
k	*kill*	To delete lines
e	*end*	To end editing with file update
q	*quit*	To end editing without file update
x	*write*	Used with r to move text lines
r	*read*	To read text lines back from disk

Using the Substitute Command

Most corrections can be quickly and accurately made by first positioning the character pointer so that the error appears in the current line. The 0lt command always moves the pointer to the beginning of the current line and then types the current line. A correction can be made with a substitute command of the form

sthat↑Zthis↑Z0lt

to substitute "this" for "that," and the result will be displayed immediately. It is important to be aware that the range of the substitute command is not limited to the current line. If by mistake we typed "thet" instead of "that," the editor would search to the end of the text buffer for "thet" and replace it, if and where found, with "this" and then display the result. One of the reasons for immediately displaying the result is to verify that the substitution occurred where intended.

On a 25-line video display screen, the command

–12L24T

can be used to advantage for a quick review in context of the result of text modification commands. On a 24-line video display, try

–12L23T

Summary

The editor provides the basic tools we need for making program pieces and putting them together, but it is not easy to master. Therefore, wherever the editor is used throughout this book, we will continue to provide detailed directions. Tedium inflicted upon the more advanced reader intent upon skimming the material will be more than amply offset by assistance rendered the beginner struggling to work the exercises exactly as suggested.

CHAPTER 3

The CP/M Debug Utility

*S*INCE DEVELOPING AN understanding of computing generally, and of CP/M specifically, is the prime objective of this book, early exposure to a computer at a rudimentary level such as that provided by the exercises in this chapter offers the best opportunity to exhibit fundamental concepts in action.

Misunderstandings about CP/M have found their way into print in more than one book. The most reliable source of information on your computer is your computer itself. To tap this source of information, you need only learn the shorthand notation known as *hexadecimal* and become familiar with a program called DDT. This chapter introduces the CP/M user to the hexadecimal number system and to CP/M's "Dynamic Debugging Tool," DDT.

The CP/M Prompt

Although we again assume that you are at the console of a CP/M system that is up and running, press Enter or Return to prove that the CP/M console command processor, CCP, is indeed running. Each time you press Enter or Return, CCP will issue its prompt. (The Enter or Return key, you will remember, is also called *carriage return*.) On most CP/M systems, the CCP prompt consists of a single letter followed by a symbol resembling an arrowhead, as follows:

A>

Although the letter is usually A, it can be any of the letters A through P. Whatever letter is used in the CCP prompt, it is the name of the current disk. If, for example, you have a two-disk system, then one disk drive is named A and the other, B. Drive A is also sometimes called Drive 0 or Unit 0, and Drive B is sometimes called Drive 1, and so on.

The CCP command

  B:

will make the disk in Drive B the current disk. The command

  A:

will restore the disk in Drive A as the current disk.

The Floppy Disk

A disk drive is a device that holds a disk and spins it around. For example, floppy disks are typically driven by an electric motor at 360 revolutions per minute. The disk drive also positions a *read–write head* over selected tracks on the disk. These tracks are concentric circles on the disk surface. The standard CP/M floppy disk has 77 tracks located in a circular band that is about an inch wide. There is room on each track of the CP/M standard 8-inch single-density disk for 26 records, each of which consists of a string of exactly 128 characters. As used in computing, the word *string* refers to a group of characters, something like a sentence except that any sequence of characters is acceptable.

The ASCII Code

The term *character* has a precise meaning in computing generally and in CP/M specifically. The characters used by CP/M are those defined by the specification called the "American Standard Code for Information Interchange," or ASCII (pronounced "ask-kee"). A table of ASCII character codes appears in Appendix A. Some ASCII characters, such as the letter A or the number 1, are printable. Others, such as carriage return, are called *control codes*, and these are not associated with a "graphic," or printable, symbol.

The ASCII specification encodes each of the 128 different characters or control codes into a unique pattern of seven bits. Just as the decimal digit is an entity that can take on one of ten values—0, 1, 2, 3, 4, 5, 6, 7, 8, or 9, exclusively— the binary digit, called a *bit*, is an entity that can take on one of two values—0 or 1, exclusively.

A physical example of something that can take on one of two values, or exist in one of two *states*, is an ordinary switch such as the toggle switch used to turn on room lights. The toggle switch can take on one of two states, "on" or "off," exclusively. These two states may be represented by the symbols 1 and 0.

The ASCII code for the letter A in binary is 0100 0001. A row of eight toggle switches could be set up to represent this character by switching six of them off and two of them on to provide the pattern 0100 0001. Notice that we have actually written a string of eight bits and that the eight bits are visually separated into two groups of four bits each. This four-bit grouping makes it easy to translate binary expressions into a convenient shorthand called *hexadecimal*.

Hexadecimal Notation

A group of four bits can take on exactly 16 different patterns. These 16 possible patterns, and a name for each pattern, are shown in Fig. 3.1.

A group of four bits is called a *hexadecimal digit*, or *hex digit*. Each hex digit has a name. The names of the hex digits are 0, 1, 2, 3, 4, 5, 6, 7, 8, 9, A, B, C, D, E, and F. Hex is a convenient shorthand for concisely expressing binary values.

The 8080/8085 and Z80 microcomputers used by CP/M process data in eight-bit *bytes*. Eight toggle switches could therefore hold one byte of information represented by two hex digits.

Binary values, of course, can also be expressed in decimal. The binary value 0100 0001 is 65 in decimal. The same binary value, expressed in hexadecimal, is 41. Conversion of binary to and from decimal is a tedious job best done by a machine, but conversion of binary to and from hexadecimal can be done instantly by eye. That is why computer programmers use hexadecimal instead of decimal to represent binary patterns such as computer memory locations, computer instructions, and the ASCII character codes.

A Debugging Example

That will be enough theory for now. Let's write a program. The first thing we have to decide is a name for it. Let's name this program HELLO.ASM. Check first to make sure that this name isn't already in use. To make this check, use the command

> DIR *.ASM

followed by carriage return, of course. CCP will display all of the existing file names that end with .ASM. If HELLO.ASM is not among them, we can use it as our name.

Binary pattern	Name
0000	0
0001	1
0010	2
0011	3
0100	4
0101	5
0110	6
0111	7
1000	8
1001	9
1010	A
1011	B
1100	C
1101	D
1110	E
1111	F

Fig. 3.1 *Hexadecimal names for binary patterns*

```
;File:  HELLO.ASM
;
        ORG     0100H
;
        MVI C,9         ;Ask for name
        LXI D,ASK
        CALL 5
;
        MVI C,10        ;Read the name
        LXI D,BUF
        CALL 5
;
;       Put a space between "Hi" and the person's name.
;
        LXI H,BUF
        MVI M,20H       ;ASCII space, or blank
        INX H
        MOV E,M         ;Get number of characters in answer
        MVI M,20H
        MVI D,0
        INX H
        DAD D
        MVI M,'!'
        INX H
        MVI M,'$'
;
        MVI C,9         ;Say "Hi"
        LXI D,ANS
        CALL 5
;
        JMP 0000        ;Return to CCP
;
ASK:    DB 'What is your name? $'
ANS:    DB 0DH,0AH,'Hi'
BUF:    DB 65   ;Buffer size is 65 characters
```

Fig. 3.2 *Assembly language text for HELLO*

Assuming that we've settled on HELLO.ASM as the name of our new program file, call the editor with the command

ED HELLO.ASM

CCP will load and start the editor, and then the editor will display the message NEW FILE followed by an asterisk (*) to show that it is in command-mode. Put the editor into input-mode with an i command followed by carriage return. The editor will advance the display to a new line and wait for input. While it is in input-mode, typing errors can be corrected by backspacing and retyping. Backspacing is effected by Rubout or Delete on most system consoles. You can backspace over line boundaries and use Control-R at any time to redisplay the current line and thus verify the position of the text pointer.

Some CP/M systems have had a problem in handling backspace on video display terminals. This problem has caused extra confusion in the editor because the editor handles backspace during input-mode differently than it does during command-mode. Anytime backspacing creates confusion, use Control-R to review the current line and the current position of the text pointer.

Using the tab key to create indenting, type in the program text shown in Fig. 3.2. Then get out of input-mode with Control-Z, and end the edit session with the E command.

We can now assemble the program. To do so, wait for the CCP prompt and then use the command

ASM HELLO

If the assembler detects any errors in our *source program*—that is, the file we have created called HELLO.ASM—it will display on the screen each source line that contains an error. If there are any assembly errors, we will have to correct the source program in the file HELLO.ASM. To do so if your system has a printer, you may first create on paper an "assembly listing" of HELLO by using the command

PIP PRN:=HELLO.PRN

The file named HELLO.PRN is a "print" file created by the assembler, ASM. In this print file, the assembler "flags" any line containing an error by putting an error code at the start, or left end, of the line. An example of a listing containing an error is shown in Fig. 3.3. The line flagged with the error code S contains the instruction MVO. MVO is not a recognizable instruction to ASM. The instruction should have been MOV.

We can use the editor to correct this or any other source code error with the command

ED HELLO.ASM

```
                   ;File:   HELLO.ASM
                   ;
   0100                     ORG     0100H
                   ;
   0100 0E09                MVI C,9         ;Ask for name
   0102 112C01              LXI D,ASK
   0105 CD0500              CALL 5
                   ;
   0108 0E0A                MVI C,10            ;Read the name
   010A 114401              LXI D,BUF
   010D CD0500              CALL 5
                   ;
                   ;       Put a space between "Hi" and the person's name.
                   ;
   0110 214401              LXI H,BUF
   0113 3620                MVI M,20H       ;ASCII space, or blank
   0115 23                  INX H
S                           MVO E,M         ;Get number of characters in answer
   0116 3620                MVI M,20H
   0118 1600                MVI D,0
   011A 23                  INX H
   011B 19                  DAD D
   011C 3621                MVI M,'!'
   011E 23                  INX H
   011F 3624                MVI M,'$'
                   ;
   0121 0E09                MVI C,9         ;Say "Hi"
   0123 114001              LXI D,ANS
   0126 CD0500              CALL 5
                   ;
   0129 C30000              JMP 0000        ;Return to CCP
                   ;
   012C 5768617420ASK:      DB 'What is your name? $'
   0140 0D0A4869  ANS:      DB 0DH,0AH,'Hi'
   0144 41        BUF:      DB 65    ;Buffer size is 65 characters
```

Fig. 3.3 *Example of a listing containing an assembly error*

We then load the entire source file into the editor's text buffer by using an append command of the form

> #A

The text pointer must now be moved to the line containing the error. To do so, either press carriage return until you reach the line of interest or use a find command of the form

> FMVO↑Z0LT

remembering to use "zero-el-tee," not "oh-el-tee."

The assembler's error flags do not appear, of course, in the source lines of the file we are editing—the source code file named HELLO.ASM. Rather, the error flag exits in the file named HELLO.PRN, the file created by the assembler.

Once the editor's text pointer is positioned at the line that contains the error, we can safely substitute MOV for MVO by using the command

> SMVO↑ZMOV↑Z0LT

Once the source file has been completely corrected, we can end the edit session with the E command.

As soon as CCP regains control, we can reassemble the program with the command

> ASM HELLO

After the editing and reassembly steps have been repeated until the assembly is error-free, we can create a command file named HELLO.COM by calling the loader with the command

> LOAD HELLO

At this point you can run your program by simply typing its name,

> HELLO

and pressing carriage return. When the program asks your name, type it in, for example,

> Jeani

and press carriage return. Your program should respond

> Hi Jean!

and then control should return to CCP.

Yes, there appears to be a bug in the program: it has lost the last character of your name! If you are interested in learning assembly language, see if you can spot this error before continuing.

The program (refer back to Fig. 3.2) appears to need an additional increment index H instruction immediately before the instruction DAD D. To make this correction, call the editor with the command

ED HELLO.ASM

When the editor responds with an asterisk (*), append the entire file—that is, load it into the text buffer with the #A command.

Now move the text pointer to the required insert position by using the find command

FDAD↑Z0LT

Then insert the new line by first putting the editor into insert-mode with the i command, followed by a carriage return, and then type in the needed instruction

INX H

followed by a carriage return, and then get out of insert-mode with Control-Z. End the edit session with the E command; then reassemble the file, load it, and test it again. The program is listed in Fig. 3.4.

In binary, the program begins at memory location 0000 0001 0000 0000. In hexadecimal, the starting location is 0100. When the program "executes," it first "points to" a text string at a location called ASK and then calls CP/M with function number 9 to display the text "What is your name?" (Function numbers are used to communicate requests to BDOS. For a definition of the CP/M function numbers, see Digital Research Manual, "CP/M 2.2 Interface Guide.") CP/M

```
                   ;File:  HELLO.ASM
                   ;
    0100                   ORG     0100H
                   ;
    0100 0E09              MVI  C,9         ;Ask for name
    0102 112D01            LXI  D,ASK
    0105 CD0500            CALL 5
                   ;
    0108 0E0A              MVI  C,10            ;Read the name
    010A 114501            LXI  D,BUF
    010D CD0500            CALL 5
                   ;
                   ;     Put a space between "Hi" and the person's name.
                   ;
    0110 214501            LXI  H,BUF
    0113 3620              MVI  M,20H        ;ASCII space, or blank
    0115 23                INX  H
    0116 5E                MOV  E,M          ;Get number of characters in answer
    0117 3620              MVI  M,20H
    0119 1600              MVI  D,0
    011B 23                INX  H
    011C 19                DAD  D
    011D 3621              MVI  M,'!'
    011F 23                INX  H
    0120 3624              MVI  M,'$'
                   ;
    0122 0E09              MVI  C,9         ;Say "Hi"
    0124 114101            LXI  D,ANS
    0127 CD0500            CALL 5
                   ;
    012A C30000            JMP  0000        ;Return to CCP
                   ;
    012D 5768617420ASK:    DB 'What is your name? $'
    0141 0D0A4869 ANS:     DB 0DH,0AH,'Hi'
    0145 41       BUF:     DB 65  ;Buffer size is 65 characters
```

Fig. 3.4 *Assembly listing of HELLO*

displays on the screen each ASCII character, starting at the location pointed to and continuing through the string of characters until it finds a dollar sign ($).

Once the question is displayed, we want to read the person's answer from the keyboard. We point to the place in the buffer called BUF to receive the typed-in answer, and we call CP/M with function number 10 to read in the answer. CP/M will read a line of text from the console keyboard and return control to location 0110 when a carriage return is typed. When control returns to this location, CP/M will have stored the answer in BUF, starting at location 0147, and the count of characters typed in will be stored in location 0146.

In order to display the word "Hi" followed by the answer, and to display the answer followed by an exclamation point character (!), we store ASCII space characters, or blanks, into the buffer-size and character-count locations, 0145 and 0146, respectively. We must retrieve the character-count from location 0146, however, before storing a blank there. We use the character count to find the end of the input string since it is there that we store the exclamation point. Finally, we store $ at the end of the string. At this point, all we have to do to create on the screen the message

Hi Jeani!

is to point to the beginning of the string at ANS and call CP/M with function code 9. The string at ANS begins with ASCII control codes 0D and 0A, expressed in hex. The pattern 0D is the code for carriage return, and the pattern 0A is the code for *line-feed*. Line-feed gets its name from the action of a printer that "feeds" the paper forward one line whenever it receives this character.

The last instruction in the program is the *jump-to-zero instruction*, JMP 0000. When HELLO runs correctly, it ends by returning control to CCP by jumping to memory location 0000.

When CCP responds with its prompt, type in the command

DIR HELLO.*

The response should be a display of file names, such as

| A: HELLO | PRN : HELLO | HEX : HELLO | ASM : HELLO | COM |
| A: HELLO | BAK : HELLO | BAS : HELLO | INT | |

The file named HELLO.ASM is the file containing the source code for our assembly language program. We created HELLO.ASM with the editor, ED, and each time we edit it, ED renames the old version of the file to save it for us. The old version of the file is named HELLO.BAK. Any previous file named HELLO.BAK is erased by the editor just before it renames HELLO.ASM.

To return to the previous version, all we have to do is erase the current version with the command

ERA HELLO.ASM

and then rename the back-up file with the command

REN HELLO.ASM=HELLO.BAK

When we call the assembler with the command

ASM HELLO

it reads the file named HELLO.ASM and creates two new files: an assembly listing in a file named HELLO.PRN and assembled machine code instructions in a file named HELLO.HEX. The latter file is displayable. To display its contents, use the command

TYPE HELLO.HEX

In response, you should get the six lines of hexadecimal digits shown in Fig. 3.5. You can also create a hardcopy listing of this file with the command

PIP LST:=HELLO.HEX

or by putting CP/M into console-print mode with Control-P before using the type command.

The file HELLO.HEX contains the machine language instructions for our program named HELLO. It is arranged for the convenience of a *loader*. A loader is a program designed to load a user's programs into memory or to create on disk an image of a user's program that can be simply copied verbatim into memory when the user calls for its execution.

Let's examine the first line of the file HELLO.HEX. The format of the hex file was designed with punched paper tape in mind. It was anticipated that the loader would read paper tape until it found a colon (:). The colon marks the beginning of a *record*. The next two hex digits following the colon give the length of the record. Our record length is 10 hex, or 16 decimal. The next four hex digits— 0100, in our case—tell the loader the starting location in memory where the machine code of the record is to be stored. The next two digits are reserved for a record-type code. Our record-type is 00. Following the code are the two hex digits 0E. This is the hexadecimal representation of the binary value

0000 1110

This binary pattern is the first machine language instruction of our program.

To an 8080 or Z80 microprocessor, the binary pattern 0000 1110 is an instruction to load the C-register with the next eight bits that follow it. The next eight bits are 0000 1001, or 09 hex. Taken together, these two eight-bit bytes, represented in hex as 0E 09, constitute an instruction that is written MVI C,9 in assembly language and is read "move immediate into C the value 9."

```
:100100000E09112D01CD05000E0A114501CD050086
:10011000214501362023 5E3620160023193621237F
:100120003624 0E09114101CD0500C3000057686156
:1001300074206 9732079 6F7572206E616D653F2040
:06014000240D0A4869418C
:0000000000
```

Fig. 3.5 *Contents of the Intel hex format file HELLO.HEX*

The next two hex digits in our record, 11, represent the machine language binary pattern

0001 0001

This is the first eight-bit byte of the three-byte instruction expressed in hex as 11 2D 01. To the 8080 or Z80, this first byte is an instruction to put the value 2D into the E-register and the value 01 into the D-register. The value 012D is the hexadecimal expression of the 16-bit address of the place in memory where the string "What is your name?" is stored. The code 11 2D 01 is the machine language representation of the assembly language instruction LXI D,ASK and is read as "Load index immediate D, with the 16-bit value defined by the location of the label symbol ASK. The register-pair, D and E taken together, is called an *index register*.

The next two hex digits, CD, represent the binary pattern

1100 1101

This binary pattern will be recognized by the 8080 as the beginning of a three-byte instruction named CALL.

When executing the CALL instruction, the 8080 will advance its program counter to point to the next byte—in our case, the byte 05. It will read this byte into the right-hand side of a temporary holding register and then advance its program counter to point to the next byte—in our case, 00. It will read this byte into the left-hand side of the holding register. The holding register now contains the 16-bit value, 0005, in hex.

To complete execution of this CALL instruction, the 8080 will advance its program counter to point to the next byte of our program. It will save the contents of the program counter in a place from which it can be easily retrieved, and then it will copy verbatim the contents of the holding register into the program counter register. In other words, the 8080 will save the address of the next instruction in our program—the instruction at location 0108—and will transfer control to location 0005, which is the entry point to CP/M.

CP/M will process the request defined by both the contents of the C-register and the contents of the DE-register-pair. After CP/M has completed processing this request, it will return control to our program; that is, it will return control to location 0108 by executing in CP/M the machine instruction

1100 1001

or C9 in hex. This instruction, written RET in assembly language, is read as "Return." The RET instruction simply retrieves the 16-bit address—0108 in our case—from where it had been saved by the CALL instruction and loads it verbatim into the 8080's program counter.

An Easier Way to Examine Machine Code

Since CP/M provides an easier way to examine machine code, let's use it. When we executed the command LOAD HELLO, the program named LOAD processed the file named HELLO.HEX and also created the executable command file named HELLO.COM from the hex format records that we have been examining.

We can examine the contents of the command file HELLO.COM by using the CP/M debug utility program, DDT. To do this, call DDT with command

      DDT HELLO.COM

After CCP loads and starts DDT, DDT will read into memory the file named HELLO.COM. The response on the screen from DDT should then be something like this:

      DDT VERS 1.4
      NEXT PC
      0180 0100

The dash (–) is DDT's prompt. NEXT refers to the hex number 0180. It means that the file HELLO.COM, when read into memory, extended from location 0100 through 017F. The next location after location 017F is location 0180. PC refers to DDT's program counter, which has been set, as indicated, to point to the start of our program at location 0100. CP/M programs always start at location 0100.

Memory Display

To see what our program looks like when loaded into memory and ready for execution, we can use DDT's display command in the form

      d100

followed by carriage return.

The display created by this command is a *hex dump* of the contents of memory starting at memory location 0100. Each line of the display exhibits the hexadecimal representation of the contents of 16 consecutive bytes of memory. Each byte of the computer's memory can store eight bits. The eight bits stored at memory location 0100 contain the binary pattern

      0000 1110

or 0E hex. This is, again, the first byte of the first instruction of our program named HELLO.

Refer to your assembly listing of HELLO or to the listing in Fig. 3.4, and compare the contents of memory, as displayed by DDT, with the machine codes printed in the listing.

The first program instruction—0E 09 or MVI C, 9—occupies bytes at locations 0100 and 0101. The second instruction—11 2D 01 or LXI D, 012D—occupies bytes at locations 0102, 0103, and 0104. The next instruction—CD 05 00 or CALL 5—occupies locations 0105, 0106, and 0107. Continue in this manner through the assembly listing to verify in memory the location of each machine instruction.

To facilitate this comparison, create a hardcopy printout of the DDT memory display by first putting CP/M into console-print mode with Control-P, and then again issue the DDT display command d100.

The last instruction of the program is C3 00 00 or JMP 0000, located in memory locations 012A, 012B, and 012C. The next byte, at memory location 012D, contains the hex value 57. From our assembly listing we can see that memory location 012D contains the first character of the string "What is your name?" The value 57 is the hexadecimal representation of the binary pattern 0101 0111, which is defined by the ASCII specification as the letter W.

Although the binary pattern 0101 0111 represents the letter W in ASCII, to an 8080 or Z80 microprocessor the binary pattern 0101 0111 represents an instruction to copy the contents of the A-register into the D-register. The thing that decides what a binary pattern represents—whether program instruction or data value—is the manner in which that byte of memory is used by your program. If, by error, your program tries to use ASCII characters as program instructions, you may be sure of unanticipated results.

Register Display

While DDT is in control, we can execute 8080 instructions one at a time and observe the results by using the DDT X command. If we type X and push carriage return, DDT should display a line something like this in response:

    C0Z0M0E0I0 A=00 B=0000 D=0000 H=0000 S=0100 P=0100 MVI C,09

C0 means that the carry flag is zero. Z0 means that the zero flag is false. M0 means that the minus flag is false. E0 means that the parity flag is not even, and I0 means that the interdigit carry is off.

Each flag consists of a single bit. The bit is a 1 if the flag is true and a 0 if it is false. These flags control the execution of some 8080 instructions. For example, the instruction C2 00 00 is something like the last instruction of our program, C3 00 00, except that C2 00 00 will "jump to 0000" only if the zero flag is false at the time the instruction is encountered. For more information on these flags see your 8080/8085 instruction guide.

To continue the explanation of the display, A=00 means that the eight-bit A-register contains binary 0000 0000, and B=0000 means that the eight-bit B-register and the eight-bit C-register each contain binary 0000 0000. Some 8080 instructions use the B and C registers together as a 16-bit *index register*. As displayed by DDT, the B-register consists of the eight bits, or two hex digits, to the left; these are called the "high-order" eight bits. Similarly, the two eight-bit registers D and E are the high and low halves of the 16-bit index register DE, and the two eight-bit registers H and L are the high and low halves of index register HL.

As we have seen, the 8080 CALL instruction stores the current contents of the program counter for later retrieval by a RET instruction. The program counter is saved by storing its 16-bit contents in two bytes of memory. The 8080 has a special register called the *stack pointer* that determines where in memory the program counter will be saved. In our DDT register display, S=0100 means that the stack pointer contains 0100. The next CALL encountered will thus save the program counter in memory locations 00FF and 00FE.

The final register displayed by DDT is the program counter register itself. P=0100 means that the program register is pointing to the first byte of the program at memory location 0100.

If the display shows that the program counter is pointing elsewhere, we can use the XP command to put 0100 into the program counter. To do so, type XP and press carriage return. When DDT responds, for example, with

P=0000

type 0100 and press carriage return; then use the X command to verify that P *does* equal 0100.

Trace

We can now use the DDT *trace command* to observe the register contents as we execute the first few instructions of the program. Each trace command will execute one 8080 instruction and immediately display the contents of the 8080 registers. Type T and press carriage return. This first trace command shows the machine state just before the first program instruction is executed. Type T and press carriage return again. This time you will see that the C-register has been loaded with the value 09. Do another trace command and you will find that the DE register pair has been loaded with the value 012D. Yet another trace command will show that the program counter has been loaded with the value 0005 and that the stack pointer has changed to 00FE.

Stack Pointer

Enter the command

DF0, 110

and press carriage return, being careful to use "zeros," not "ohs." At the right-hand end of the first hex dump line created, you will find the values 08 in memory location 00FE and 01 in memory location 00FF. They comprise the "saved" contents of the program counter that have been "pushed on the stack" by the 8080 microprocessor when it executed the CALL instruction at location 0105.

Breakpoints

We will allow CP/M to run without stopping until it has processed our requested function. To regain control when the function is done, we will "breakpoint" our program at location 0108 by typing the command

G, 108

followed by carriage return. We should get our expected message

What is your name?

followed by *0108. DDT will then display a prompt (−) to show that it has regained control. At this time we will breakpoint to location 0110 with the command

> G, 110

When we press carriage return, nothing will happen since CP/M is processing our requested function, that is, it is waiting for a line of text to be typed. We now type in a response such as Jeani, just as we did earlier, and when we press carriage return, control will come back to DDT at location 0110 in our program.

We can display the buffer with D145,14F. If we have typed Jeani, the hex dump of the buffer will look like this:

> 0145   41 05 4A 65 61 6E 69 00 00 00 00

The value 41 in location 0145 is the value we put there to define the size of our buffer for CP/M. CP/M stored the value 05 in location 0146 to show that five characters have been typed in. The five ASCII-encoded characters Jeani follow.

We can continue to step through the program with the trace command or simply allow the program to run to completion by typing G followed by carriage return.

DDT's trace feature is usable on most CP/M applications programs. Applications programs that have been written on 8085- or Z80-based systems but designed to run on all CP/M systems will necessarily be programmed in the 8080 subset of the broader 8085 or Z80 instruction sets. DDT's trace feature works only with 8080 instructions, but the breakpoint feature will work on all programs.

An Exercise

Is the following program functionally accurate?

> ORG 0100H
> DB 'Doctor, my problem is$'
> MVI C,9
> LXI D,0100h
> CALL 5
> JMP 0

Answer

When CCP starts a program, it always transfers control to location 0100. This program has ASCII characters stored at location 0100. The results generated may be different from those anticipated. To find out whether this is the case, use the editor to create this program in a file named TEST.ASM, for example, and assemble it with the command

> ASM TEST

Create the command file with

> LOAD TEST

and then load the machine code program under DDT with the command

> DDT TEST.COM

List the actual program code with the DDT command

> L100

Can you predict the results of running this program? The results generated depend on the contents of the machine registers at the time the program receives control. If we run this program under DDT, it will write into memory location 0000, which contains a jump instruction necessary for system operation. The chaos that would follow execution of this program is known as a system *crash*.

A functionally accurate version of this program would be

```
ORG 0100H
MVI C,9
LXI D,TEXT
CALL 5
JMP 0
TEXT:   DB 'Doctor, my problem is$'
```

A Question

How many toggle switches are required to store one hexadecimal digit?

Answer

One hexadecimal digit represents four bits. One toggle switch can store one bit. It therefore takes four toggle switches to store one hex digit.

Summary

In this chapter we have been introduced to the following DDT commands:

D   Display memory
G   Begin execution with optional breakpoint
L   List memory in assembler mnemonics
S   Substitute
T   Trace program execution
X   Examine registers

A brief but detailed summary of all DDT commands can be found in The Digital Research manual titled "CP/M Dynamic Debugging Tool (DDT) User's Guide."

CHAPTER 4

The ASCII Character Code

*I*N THIS CHAPTER, after we use the editor to create three files, we will use PIP to combine these three files into one. The result will provide a program that will allow us to explore the character codes actually created by the keyboard.

Creating the First File

First, determine if the three file names FILE1.TMP, FILE2.TMP, and FILE3.TMP are available. To do so, use the CCP directory command

DIR FILE?.TMP

When CP/M searches the disk directory, the ? character will be taken to represent any character occupying the fifth character position of any file name in the directory. If the response we get is

NOT FOUND

or

NO FILE

then we will know that all three of our proposed file names are available.

Assuming the availability of our three file names, or some three similar file names of your own choosing, let us create the first file. Call the editor with the command

ED FILE1.TMP

CCP will load the editor and start it running; then ED will issue the message

NEW FILE

confirming that a file by the name FILE1.TMP does not already exist. The editor will then display an asterisk (*) to show that it is in command-mode.

Type i followed by carriage return to put the editor into input-mode. Now type the text shown in Fig. 4.1. Use the tab key for indenting. Each line ends with a carriage return. Note that 100H is "one-zero-zero" not "one-oh-oh," a remark that also applies to JZ 0000.

When you have completed typing the text, take the editor out of input-mode with Control-Z; then end the edit session with the E command. We have now created the first of our three files.

To display the contents of this file, use the CCP type command

TYPE FILE1.TMP

Creating the Second File

Since we are now ready to create the second of our three files, we call the editor with the command

ED FILE2.TMP

Again, we should get the response NEW FILE followed by an asterisk when the editor is ready for a command. Put the editor into input-mode with an i command, and type the program text shown in Fig. 4.2.

After typing this text, take the editor out of input-mode with Control-Z. Move the text pointer to the beginning of the text buffer with the B command. Push carriage return repeatedly to display the text and advance the text pointer

```
;         ASCII - Display ASCII codes in hexadecimal.
;
          ORG 100H
ASC:      CALL ALN         ;Advance to new line
          CALL RCC         ;Read a character
          CPI 3
          JZ 0000          ;If control-C
;
          PUSH PSW
          CALL RLN         ;Restore line
          CALL FCC         ;Filter control-codes
          CALL DCH         ;"echo" the character
          MOV A,B
          CALL DCH
          CALL ISM         ;Say "is encoded as"
          POP PSW
          CALL DHB         ;Display it in hex
          JMP ASC          ;Loop
;
;         ISM - Issue message: "is encoded as"
;
ISM:      LXI D,ISMA
          CALL MSG
          RET
;
ISMA:     DB        is encoded (in hex) as: $'
```

Fig. 4.1 Text for ASCII main program

```
;
;           FCC - Filter out Control Codes.
;           Entry   A = ASCII code
;           Exit    B = ASCII graphic char
;                   A = 'up-arrow' if control-code
;                     = blank, if graphic
;
FCC:        CPI 20H
            JNC FCC1        ;If not control code
;
;           We have a control-code.
;           Return 'up-arrow' in A; graphic in B.
;
            ADI 40H
            MOV B,A
            MVI A,5EH       ;up-arrow
            RET
;
;           We have a graphic character.
;           Return blank in A; graphic in B.
;
FCC1:       MOV B,A
            MVI A,20H       ;blank
            RET
;
;           MSG - Issue Message to Console.
;           Entry   DE = message address
;
MSG:        MVI C,9
            CALL 5
            RET
;
;           RCC - Read a Console Character.
;           Exit    A = character
;
RCC:        MVI C,1
            CALL 5
            RET
```

Fig. 4.2 *Text for subroutines FCC, MSG, and RCC*

line-by-line. Use the T command to redisplay the current line—that is, the line to which the text pointer is currently pointing. The current line will be displayed each time you enter a T command. If you use the command 4T, it will display four lines, but if you use it again, you will get the same four lines. The T command does not move the text pointer.

Correcting Invisible Errors

Occasionally, a control-code may be imbedded in the text because of a keyboard error. The editor displays these otherwise invisible codes by converting them for display purposes into two characters, an up-arrow followed by a displayable character. If while typing a line of text in input-mode you hold down the control key and press b, for example, nothing will be displayed and the error may therefore go undetected. If the editor is made to display the text, however—by Control-R, for example—the imbedded control code will be revealed. Imbedded control codes can be backspaced over if you catch the error while typing the line. If you find the error later, you must make that line the current line and delete it entirely with 1k. Then go into input-mode with i followed by carriage return, retype the line followed by carriage return, and then go back to command-mode with Control-Z.

You can move the text pointer backward toward the beginning of the text buffer by using the L command in the form −5L, for example.

When you are satisfied that the text in the file is the same as the text in the book, end the edit session with the E command. You can always review the contents of a text file like this one by using a CCP type command such as

TYPE FILE2.TMP

On a newly typed file such as this, however, it is always preferable to review the file first by using the editor itself. The editor "filters out" imbedded control codes and visibly displays them. Depending on the construction of your console terminal, CCP's TYPE command will at best ignore imbedded control codes. Some "smart" terminals may reconfigure themselves or perform other unexpected operations if control codes are imbedded in the text transmitted for display.

Creating the Third File

We are ready now to create our third file. Call the editor with the command

ED FILE3.TMP

The editor should confirm that this is a NEW FILE and then display a command-mode prompt (*). Put the editor into input-mode with i followed by carriage return. Type in the text shown in Fig. 4.3.

After typing the last line of text, take the editor out of input-mode with Control-Z. Move the text pointer to the top of the text buffer with the B command. Type out the entire text with the #T command. Stop and start the scrolling of the display with Control-S. If there are no imbedded control codes and the text appears to be an accurate copy of the text in the book, then end the edit session with the E command.

When CCP regains control, use the directory command

DIR FILE?.TMP

to confirm that there are indeed three files that now satisfy this ambiguous request. You should now have on the disk FILE1.TMP, FILE2.TMP, and FILE3.TMP.

Merging Files

We can now use the Peripheral Interchange Program, PIP, to create one large file from these three smaller files. Since this new large file is to be processed by the assembler, the name we give it must end with .ASM to indicate its file type. An appropriate name might be ASCII.ASM.

To determine if ASCII.ASM is available, use the directory command

DIR ASCII.ASM

The response we want is NO FILE or NOT FOUND.

```
;
;              DHB - Display Hex Byte.
;              Display two hex digits.
;              Entry   A = byte to be displayed
;
DHB:     PUSH PSW
         RRC ! RRC ! RRC ! RRC
         CALL DHD          ;display hex digit
         POP PSW
;
;              DHD - Display Hex Digit.
;              Entry   A,low 4 bits = digit
;
DHD:     ANI 0FH
         CPI 10
         JNC DHD1          ;If not 0 through 9
;
         ADI '0'
         JMP DCH
;
DHD1:    ADI 'A'-10        ;Create "A,B,C,D,E, or F"
;
;              DCH - Display one character.
;              Entry   A = ASCII encoded char
;
DCH:     PUSH B
         MOV E,A
         MVI C,2
         CALL 5
         POP B
         RET
;
;              RLN - Restore line.
;              Save char, and restore to column one.
;
RLN:     MOV B,A
         CALL ALN1         ;issue carriage-return
         MOV A,B
         RET
;
;              ALN - Advance to new line.
;              Issue CR,LF
;
ALN:     MVI A,0AH         ;line-feed
         CALL DCH
ALN1:    MVI A,0DH         ;carriage-return
         CALL DCH
         RET
```

Fig. 4.3 Text for subroutines DHB, DHD, DCH, RLN, and ALN

Using ASCII.ASM or any other available name that ends with .ASM, merge the three smaller files into one large file with the command

PIP ASCII.ASM=FILE1.TMP,FILE2.TMP,FILE3.TMP

When CCP regains control following this operation, display the new file with

TYPE ASCII.ASM

and verify that ASCII.ASM is indeed a concatenation of the three small files. Use Control-S to stop and start scrolling of the display.

Assembling and Testing

Assemble the new program with the command

ASM ASCII

If there are assembly errors, print out the assembly listing with the command

PIP PRN:=ASCII.PRN

To find what needs to be corrected, carefully compare your listing with the assembly listing in Fig. 4.4. To correct any assembly errors, call the editor with the command

ED ASCII.ASM

Bring the entire file into the text buffer with the #A command, and then correct the text. End the edit session with the E command, and then reassemble the program with the command

```
                    ;        ASCII - Display ASCII codes in hexadecimal.
                    ;
     0100                    ORG 100H
     0100 CD8501    ASC:     CALL ALN        ;Advance to new line
     0103 CD5901             CALL RCC        ;Read a character
     0106 FE03               CPI 3
     0108 CA0000             JZ 0000         ;If control-C
                    ;
     010B F5                 PUSH PSW
     010C CD7F01             CALL RLN        ;Restore line
     010F CD4401             CALL FCC        ;Filter control-codes
     0112 CD7601             CALL DCH        ;"echo" the character
     0115 78                 MOV A,B
     0116 CD7601             CALL DCH
     0119 CD2301             CALL ISM        ;Say "is encoded as"
     011C F1                 POP PSW
     011D CD5F01             CALL DHB        ;Display it in hex
     0120 C30001             JMP ASC         ;Loop
                    ;
                    ;        ISM - Issue message: "is encoded as"
                    ;
     0123 112A01    ISM:     LXI D,ISMA
     0126 CD5301             CALL MSG
     0129 C9                 RET
                    ;
     012A 2069732065ISMA:    DB       ' is encoded (in hex) as: $'
                    ;
                    ;        FCC - Filter out Control Codes.
                    ;        Entry   A = ASCII code
                    ;        Exit    B = ASCII graphic char
                    ;                A = 'up-arrow' if control-code
                    ;                  = blank, if graphic
                    ;
     0144 FE20      FCC:     CPI 20H
     0146 D24F01             JNC FCC1        ;If not control code
                    ;
                    ;        We have a control-code.
                    ;        Return 'up-arrow' in A; graphic in B.
                    ;
     0149 C640               ADI 40H
     014B 47                 MOV B,A
     014C 3E5E               MVI A,5EH       ;up-arrow
     014E C9                 RET
                    ;
                    ;        We have a graphic character.
                    ;        Return blank in A; graphic in B.
                    ;
     014F 47        FCC1:    MOV B,A
     0150 3E20               MVI A,20H       ;blank
     0152 C9                 RET
                    ;
                    ;        MSG - Issue Message to Console.
                    ;        Entry   DE = message address
                    ;
```

Fig. 4.4 *Assembly listing of ASCII display program*

```
0153 0E09        MSG:     MVI C,9
0155 CD0500               CALL 5
0158 C9                   RET
                 ;
                 ;        RCC - Read a Console Character.
                 ;        Exit    A = character
                 ;
0159 0E01        RCC:     MVI C,1
015B CD0500               CALL 5
015E C9                   RET
                 ;
                 ;        DHB - Display Hex Byte.
                 ;        Display two hex digits.
                 ;        Entry   A = byte to be displayed
                 ;
015F F5          DHB:     PUSH PSW
0160 0F0F0F0F             RRC ! RRC ! RRC ! RRC
0164 CD6801               CALL DHD        ;display hex digit
0167 F1                   POP PSW
                 ;
                 ;        DHD - Display Hex Digit.
                 ;        Entry   A,low 4 bits = digit
                 ;
0168 E60F        DHD:     ANI 0FH
016A FE0A                 CPI 10
016C D27401               JNC DHD1        ;If not 0 through 9
                 ;
016F C630                 ADI '0'
0171 C37601               JMP DCH
                 ;
0174 C637        DHD1:    ADI 'A'-10      ;Create "A,B,C,D,E, or F"
                 ;
                 ;        DCH - Display one character.
                 ;        Entry   A = ASCII encoded char
                 ;
0176 C5          DCH:     PUSH B
0177 5F                   MOV E,A
0178 0E02                 MVI C,2
017A CD0500               CALL 5
017D C1                   POP B
017E C9                   RET
                 ;
                 ;        RLN - Restore line.
                 ;        Save char, and restore to column one.
                 ;
017F 47          RLN:     MOV B,A
0180 CD8A01               CALL ALN1       ;issue carriage-return
0183 78                   MOV A,B
0184 C9                   RET
                 ;
                 ;        ALN - Advance to new line.
                 ;        Issue CR,LF
                 ;
0185 3E0A        ALN:     MVI A,0AH       ;line-feed
0187 CD7601               CALL DCH
018A 3E0D        ALN1:    MVI A,0DH       ;carriage-return
018C CD7601               CALL DCH
018F C9                   RET
```

Fig. 4.4 Assembly listing of ASCII display program (Cont.)

ASM ASCII

When you achieve an error-free assembly, you can create the command file ASCII.COM by calling the loader with the command

LOAD ASCII

Then execute the program with the command

ASCII

This program should respond to each key pressed on the keyboard. Each time you press a key, your program should respond with a line such as

A is encoded (in hex) as 41

Summary

In this chapter we have developed a program with which you can display the ASCII code for nearly all the letters and control codes that your keyboard is capable of generating. Use this program to test all keys on your keyboard, including all shift, control, and control-shift combinations. Control-C is the only code this program will not display since it is used to control the program itself. When the program detects the Control-C ASCII code (03), it jumps to memory location 0000 in CP/M and thereby returns control to CCP.

5

The Console Command Processor

*T*HE FIRST PURPOSE of the exercise in this chapter is to fix in mind clearly the distinction between *built-in commands* and *transient commands*. We will then write a small program and use it to examine the CP/M mechanism that passes command information to a transient program.

Testing the DIR Command

Call DDT with the command

>   *DDT*

Clear one *page* (256 bytes) of memory at location 0100 with the command

>   *F100,1FF,0*

This "fills" memory from 0100 through 01FF—one page—with 00. Get out of DDT with G0 or Control-C.

Call for a directory display with the CCP command

>   *DIR*

Now save the memory page at 0100 with the command

>   *SAVE 1 IMAGE.COM*

This copies to disk an image of memory from 0100 through 01FF. In place of IMAGE you can use any available name you wish. Load the saved memory image along with DDT by using the command

DDT IMAGE.COM

This restores memory from 0100 through 01FF to the exact state it was in immediately after the DIR command completed processing. Display this memory state as left by DIR with the DDT command

D100

You should find that memory starting at location 0100 was in no way modified by the DIR command. The page at 0100 should still be filled with 00. In other words, the CCP directory command did not cause any portion of a program or anything else to be loaded into this portion of the transient program area.

Testing the Type Command

Get out of DDT with G0 or Control-C. Display the contents of the file ASCII.ASM with the CCP command

TYPE ASCII.ASM

Again, save the residue left by the processing of this command by using the CCP command

SAVE 1 IMAGE.COM

Load the saved image along with DDT by the command

DDT IMAGE.COM

Verify that the first page of the transient program area starting at 0100 was again not modified by the TYPE command. The TYPE command, like the DIR command, does not use or modify the transient program area.

Testing the STAT Command

Get out of DDT with G0 or Control-C. Display the amount of disk space available on the current disk by using the command

STAT

Save an image of any residue left in the first page of the transient program area by using the command

SAVE 1 IMAGE.COM

Load the image under DDT with the command

DDT IMAGE.COM

You should find that the command STAT, a transient command, has modified the transient program area. STAT, ED, ASM, HELLO, SUBMIT, and indeed all such user programs cause code to be loaded into the transient program area.

Built-In Commands

The commands DIR and TYPE are examples of built-in commands. Built-in commands are processed entirely by programs that reside in CCP. The processing of a CCP built-in command does *not* modify the transient program area. CCP has built-in commands for the following operations:

DIR afn	To display filenames
TYPE ufn	To display ASCII files
SAVE ufn	To save memory starting at 0100
REN new=old	To rename a file
ERA afn	To delete files
d:	To set current disk equal to d
USER n	To set CP/M 2.2 user number

The functions available under the first six of these commands—the CP/M 1.4 subset—are discussed in detail in the Digital Research manual, "An Introduction to CP/M Features and Facilities." For a discussion of the USER command, see the Digital Research manual, "CP/M 2.2 User's Guide."

Zero Length File Trick

Create a file of zero length with the command

SAVE 0 RUTHERE.COM

This creates a directory entry for the file RUTHERE.COM but writes nothing into the file. The CCP command

RUTHERE

will now cause CCP to load nothing into memory, starting at location 0100, and thus re-execute whatever program was last loaded into the transient program area.

For the following exercise, we need the program listed in Fig. 5.1. Use the command

DIR IAMHERE.ASM

to verify the availability of the file name IAMHERE.ASM, or invent a file name of your own, remembering that the name must end with .ASM. If you select a name other than IAMHERE, use that name throughout this exercise wherever IAMHERE appears.

Call the editor with the command

ED IAMHERE.ASM

```
;File:    IAMHERE.ASM
;
;         Test the "built-in" commands.
;
          ORG 100H
;
          LXI D,MSG
          MVI C,9
          CALL 5
          RET
;
MSG:      DB       'I am still here.$'
```

Fig. 5.1 *Text for IAMHERE*

The editor should respond NEW FILE and then display a command-mode prompt (*). Put the editor into input-mode with i followed by carriage return. Then type the text shown in Fig. 5.1.

After typing the carriage return at the end of the last line of text, get out of input-mode with Control-Z. Move the character pointer to the beginning of the text with the B command. Display the entire file with the #T command. Verify that your text is the same as that in Fig. 5.1, and then end the edit session with the E command.

Assemble your program with the command

ASM IAMHERE

If there are any assembly errors, then display the assembly listing with the command

TYPE IAMHERE.PRN

and carefully compare your listing with the assembly listing of IAMHERE in Fig. 5.2. To correct any typing errors, call the editor with the command

ED IAMHERE.ASM

Bring the entire source file into memory with the #A command. Use the edit commands to correct the text, and then end the edit session with the E command.

Reassemble your program with the command.

ASM IAMHERE

```
                    ;File:    IAMHERE.ASM
                    ;
                    ;         Test the "built-in" commands.
                    ;
0100                          ORG 100H
                    ;
0100 110901                   LXI D,MSG
0103 0E09                     MVI C,9
0105 CD0500                   CALL 5
0108 C9                       RET
                    ;
0109 4920616D20MSG:           DB       'I am still here.$'
```

Fig. 5.2 *Assembly listing of IAMHERE*

When you have an error-free assembly, create the command file IAMHERE.COM by calling the loader with the command

>*LOAD IAMHERE*

Tests to Show Which Commands Are Built In

Call your program with the command

>*IAMHERE*

Your program should respond by displaying the message "I am still here." We can now test the transient program area to see if our program is still there by using the command

>*RUTHERE*

Since RUTHERE is a file of zero length, it causes CCP to re-execute whatever is in the transient program area. We should again get the response "I am still here."

Display the disk directory with the command

>*DIR*

Check the TPA with the command

>*RUTHERE*

Create a file with the command

>*SAVE 9 TEMP.TMP*

Test the TPA with the command

>*RUTHERE*

Rename the file with the command

>*REN TEST.XXX=TEMP.TMP*

Check the TPA with the command

>*RUTHERE*

Erase the file with the command

>*ERA TEST.XXX*

Check the TPA with the command

>*RUTHERE*

Display your assembly listing with the command

>*TYPE IAMHERE.PRN*

Test the TPA with the command

RUTHERE

Display disk status with the command

STAT

Check the TPA with the command

RUTHERE

DIR, SAVE, REN, ERA, and TYPE are built-in CCP commands. STAT, however, is a transient command.

Processing Transient Commands

The processing of a transient command begins when CCP detects that the command received from the console keyboard is not a built-in command. For example, when CCP determines that the command

STAT

doesn't match any of the names in its table of built-in commands, CCP will form a file name by appending .COM to the command, thus creating, in this example, the file name STAT.COM. A search of the disk will then be made for a file of this name. If a file by this name exists on the disk, then CCP will copy the file verbatim into memory starting at location 0100.

After the file has been copied into memory, CCP will execute the instruction

CALL 0100

to give control of the computer to the program that is assumed to have been loaded by the verbatim copy operation. All commands to CCP that are not built-in commands are processed in this manner. Under CP/M, *all* programs are executed as transient commands.

Passing Information to a Called Program

When CCP loads a transient program, it can "pass" to that program the name or names of one or more files. In this section we will perform an exercise enabling us to examine the mechanism used by CCP to pass file names and other information to a called program, and, in the process, we will get our first glimpse into the data structure of the CP/M file processing system.

One of CCP's main jobs is to load user programs into the transient program area, called the *TPA*. The TPA begins at 0100 and extends to the first word address (fwa) of CCP itself. After a user program is loaded, it can, if necessary, use the memory space that was occupied by CCP. In a sense, therefore, CCP occupies a portion of the TPA. CP/M occupies all of the memory below and above the

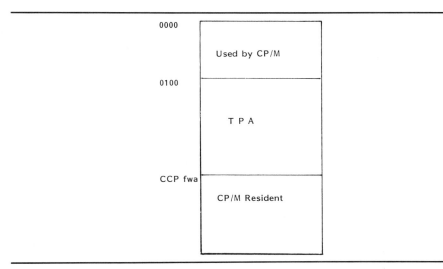

Fig. 5.3 CP/M memory map with location 0000 at top

TPA. This CP/M memory allocation scheme is illustrated in Fig. 5.3. The same information is illustrated again in Fig. 5.4, rearranged so that the "top," or high address portion, of memory is at the top of the illustration. Such illustrations of memory allocation are called *memory maps*.

The CP/M "resident" always occupies the top of available memory. We eventually will explore the CP/M resident, but our immediate objective is to discover what is going on in the area that is always reserved by CP/M at locations 0000 through 00FF. To assist this investigation, we will write a small program named MOVE9.

Use a directory command in the form

> DIR MOVE9.*

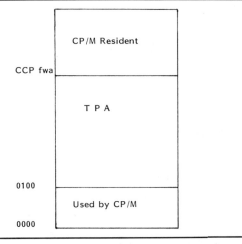

Fig. 5.4 CP/M memory map with location 0000 at bottom

to assure that the name MOVE9 is not already in use. If it is, you will have to invent some other name for this program. The purpose of the program is to "move," or copy, the contents of memory locations 0000 through 00FF into a buffer starting at memory location 0900. *Buffer* is a buzz word. It simply means a place in memory to store something.

Call the editor with the command

ED MOVE9.ASM

The editor should respond with NEW FILE and then a command-mode prompt (*). Put the editor into input-mode with i followed by carriage return. Type in the text shown in Fig. 5.5. Follow each line with a carriage return. After typing the last line, get out of input-mode with Control-Z, and then end the edit session with the E command.

Assemble your new program with the command

ASM MOVE9

The assembler will read the source file MOVE9.ASM and create the Intel format hex file MOVE9.HEX and the assembly listing file MOVE9.PRN.

During the assembly process, the assembler will display on the screen any line of the source file containing text whose meaning is not recognizable by the assembler. If there are any assembly errors, print out the assembly listing with the command

PIP PRN:=MOVE9.PRN

and then carefully compare your assembly listing with the assembly listing in Fig. 5.6. Then edit the source file and reassemble it.

Once you have an error-free assembly, you can create the command file MOVE9.COM by calling the loader with the command

```
;File:   MOVE9.ASM
;
;
;
        ORG 100H
        LXI H,0000H
        LXI D,0900H
        LXI B,-256      ;-byte count
;
;       MMV - Move Memory.
;       Entry   HL = Source fwa
;               DE = Destination fwa
;               BC = - byte count
;
MMV:    MOV A,M
        STAX D
        INX H
        INX D
        INR C
        JNZ MMV         ;If not done
;
        INR B
        JNZ MMV         ;If not done
        RET
```

Fig. 5.5 Text for MOVE9

```
                          ;File:   MOVE9.ASM
                          ;
                          ;
                          ;
          0100                     ORG 100H
          0100  210000             LXI H,0000H
          0103  110009             LXI D,0900H
          0106  0100FF             LXI B,-256      ;-byte count
                          ;
                          ;        MMV - Move Memory.
                          ;        Entry   HL = Source fwa
                          ;                DE = Destination fwa
                          ;                BC = - byte count
                          ;
          0109  7E        MMV:     MOV A,M
          010A  12                 STAX D
          010B  23                 INX H
          010C  13                 INX D
          010D  0C                 INR C
          010E  C20901             JNZ MMV         ;If not done
                          ;
          0111  04                 INR B
          0112  C20901             JNZ MMV         ;If not done
          0115  C9                 RET
```

Fig. 5.6 Assembly listing of MOVE9

LOAD MOVE9

Load the new program under DDT with the command

DDT MOVE9.COM

When DDT displays its prompt (–), verify that MOVE9.COM has indeed been loaded into memory at location 0100 by listing the program with the DDT command

L100,115

The result should be a display like that in Fig. 5.7.

Type an X followed by carriage return to display the computer registers. Verify that the program counter has been preset to 0100. The display line created by the X command should include the entry P=0100. The program counter can be set, if necessary, by typing XP followed by carriage return and then typing 0100 followed by another carriage return.

We will now execute the first three instructions of MOVE9 and then check the computer registers. To do so, we will use a "go with breakpoint" command in the form

```
          0100  LXI   H,0000
          0103  LXI   D,0900
          0106  LXI   B,FF00
          0109  MOV   A,M
          010A  STAX  D
          010B  INX   H
          010C  INX   D
          010D  INR   C
          010E  JNZ   0109
          0111  INR   B
          0112  JNZ   0109
          0115  RET
```

Fig. 5.7 Disassembly listing of MOVE9

>   *G,109*

When DDT stops the program at location 0109, it will display *0109. Now type X followed by carriage return. Verify that the HL register contains zero—H=0000—that the DE register contains 0900—D=0900—and that the BC register contains FF00—B=FF00.

Now breakpoint to location 010E with the command

>   *G,10E*

followed by carriage return. When DDT responds with *010E, type X followed by carriage return. Verify that the BC register contains FF01.

Breakpoint to location 0112. Verify that the BC register contains 0000. Display memory locations 0000 through 007F with the command

>   *D0,7F*

Dump memory locations 0900 through 097F with the command

>   *D900,97F*

Verify that the contents of memory starting at location 0900 are identical to the contents of memory starting at location 0000. Then get out of DDT with Control-C or G0.

Control-C causes CP/M to jump to 0000. The DDT command G0 causes DDT to jump to 0000. Either command produces the same result. Memory location 0000 contains a jump to a program that is part of the CP/M resident. The purpose of that program, called the *warmboot loader,* is to return control of the computer to CCP—if necessary, by reloading CCP from the disk.

When CCP regains control of the computer, it will display the *system prompt,* which contains a letter that is the name of the current disk and an arrowhead-shaped symbol such as

>   *A>*

When CCP regains control, call your program with the command

>   *MOVE9*

CCP will load and start MOVE9. MOVE9 runs and returns quickly to CCP without going through the warmboot processor. When control returns to CCP, save the result created by MOVE9 with the command

>   *SAVE 9 IMAGE.COM*

Now load the saved image with the command

>   *DDT IMAGE.COM*

Display memory at location 0900 with the DDT command

>   *D900,9FF*

followed by carriage return. The contents of memory locations 0900 through 09FF are a verbatim image of memory locations 0000 through 00FF as they existed at the time that MOVE9 gained control of the computer. For example, the instruction occupying locations 0900, 0901, and 0902 is a copy of the jump instruction that occupies locations 0000, 0001, and 0002. This instruction provides, as we have seen, a linkage between user programs and the CP/M program that is used to reload and restart CCP.

The instruction occupying memory locations 0905, 0906, and 0907 is an image of the jump instruction that occupies locations 0005, 0006, and 0007. The jump at 0005 provides, as we have seen, a linkage between user programs and the CP/M program that manages the computer system. All CP/M user programs, including ED, ASM, LOAD, and STAT, communicate with CP/M through the BDOS *vector* at memory location 0005 (a *vector* is a jump instruction). The vector at 0005 is a jump to the basic disk operation system program called BDOS.

The Way CCP Handles File Names

Get out of DDT with Control-C and then call MOVE9 with a command that includes an *argument*, such as

> *MOVE9 MYFILE.XXX*

Again, save the result with

> *SAVE 9 IMAGE.COM*

Call DDT with

> *DDT IMAGE.COM*

Display memory from 0900 through 09FF with

> *D900,9FF*

Examine the contents of memory locations 095C through 096A with the DDT command

> *D95C,96A*

These locations should contain the bytes

> *00 4D 59 46 49 4C 45 20 20 58 58 58 00 00 00*

This is the ASCII encoded file name MYFILE.XXX arranged in CP/M *file control block format*. A CP/M file name always contains eight characters. Therefore, CCP has appended two ASCII blanks (20) to the six-character name MYFILE. The three-character ASCII-encoded file type XXX follows the eight-character file name. The term *file name* is sometimes used to indicate the 11-character concatenation of file name and file type. The CP/M file type always consists of three characters.

Fill the *default file control block* at 005C and the *default buffer* at 0080 with hexadecimal FF by using the DDT command

F5C,FF,FF

CCP Formats Up to Two File Names

Then get out of DDT with Control-C. Call MOVE9 with the command

MOVE9 MYFILE.X YOURFILE.Y

Save the result with

SAVE 9 IMAGE.COM

Load the image under DDT with

DDT IMAGE.COM

Use the DDT command

D95C,97B

to examine the bytes that MOVE9 found starting at location 005C. You should find the formatted file name MYFILE.X starting at location 095D and the formatted file name YOURFILE.Y starting at location 096D. The single-letter file types will have been padded to three characters with ASCII blanks. Memory locations not written into by CCP will still contain FF.

Passing the Entire Command

Get out of DDT with Control-C and call MOVE9 with the command

MOVE9 MYFILE.XXX YOURFILE.YYY (AND LET'S SEE WHERE HE PUTS THIS.)

Save the result with

SAVE 9 IMAGE.COM

and then call DDT with

DDT IMAGE.COM

Display memory from 095C through 09BF with

D95C,9BF

and verify not only that CCP passed to MOVE9 two file names arranged in file control block format at locations 005C and 006C, but also that it placed nearly the entire command text line in the buffer starting at location 0080. The value (3D hex, or 61) stored in memory location 0080, or at 0980 in the image, is the count of characters in the buffer. Figure 5.8 is a partially "interpreted" version of the memory at location 005C as it would have been found by MOVE9.

The Drive Prefix

Get out of DDT with G0 or Control-C. Call MOVE9 with the command

MOVE9 B:MYFILE.XXX C:YOURFILE.YYY

Save the image and examine it with DDT. Verify that MOVE9 found that the prefix B: was translated into the hex value 02 and stored at location 005C. Verify that the prefix C: was translated into the hex value 03 and stored at location 006C. A file name prefix such as this, called a *drive prefix*, is used to designate a disk drive for the named file.

Throughout CP/M, wherever a file name is used, a drive prefix can designate the disk drive to which the named file is to be written or from which the named file is to be read. For example, assuming that your system has disk drives B and C, the CCP command

B:DDT C:TEST.COM

will cause CCP to load DDT from the file DDT.COM on the disk in drive B. DDT will then load the program named TEST from the file TEST.COM on the disk in drive C.

Some commands use a prefix alone to designate a disk drive. For example, the CCP command

DIR B:

creates a display of the directory of the disk in drive B.

When a string such as B:MYFILE.XXX has been analyzed, translated, and reformatted, it is said to have been *parsed*.

When CCP processes a program call command, it will parse two file names and place them in file control block format at 005C and 006C. It will also place nearly the entire command line into a buffer at 0080 where it can be further analyzed, if necessary, by the called program.

First Exercise

Display disk status with the command

STAT

```
005C  00  M  Y  F  I  L  E 20 20  X  X  X 00 00 00 xx
006C  00  Y  O  U  R  F  I  L  E  Y  Y  Y 00 00 00 xx
007C  00 xx xx xx
0080  3D 20  M  Y  F  I  L  E  .  X  X  X 20  Y  O  U
0090  R  F  I  L  E  .  Y  Y  Y 20  (  A  N  D 20  L
00A0  E  T  '  S 20  S  E  E 20  W  H  E  R  E 20  H
00B0  E 20  P  U  T  S 20  T  H  I  S  .  ) 00 xx xx
```

Fig. 5.8 *Examples of parameters and parsed file names passed by CCP to a called transient program*

Warmboot your system with Control-C. Test the TPA with the command

>   *RUTHERE*

Since warmboot does not modify the transient program area, STAT should still be there.

Second Exercise

Call STAT with the command

>   *STAT *.ASM*

Display the directory with the command

>   *DIR*

Show that STAT is still present in the TPA by using your restart command

>   *RUTHERE*

You should find that STAT indeed is still present but that the argument *.ASM has been lost.

Try the command

>   *RUTHERE *.ASM*

Now try the command

>   *RUTHERE *.COM*

The buffers used to pass arguments through CCP to called transient programs are not in the TPA; they will be used anew by every command to CCP.

Summary

In this chapter we've demonstrated the fundamental difference between built-in commands and transient commands. A transient command is executed by loading a program into the user portion of memory, called the *transient program area*. This, of course, modifies the transient program area. Built-in commands do not use or modify the transient program area.

The Disk
File Directory

*T*HE FIRST PROGRAM that we will write in this chapter counts all occurrences in the CP/M file directory of the thoroughly ambiguous file name *.*. Then we will create a second program that counts all occurrences of any file that we specify by name in the program call command. A by-product of this exercise provides an introduction to the CP/M file directory.

Creating a Subroutine Library

Use a directory command in the form

> *DIR *.TMP*

to verify the existence of the three files FILE1.TMP, FILE2.TMP, and FILE3.TMP. These files were developed by the exercises described in Chap. 4. Display the contents of FILE1.TMP with the command

> *TYPE FILE1.TMP*

and verify that this is indeed the file created by the exercise described in Chap. 4. Do the same for FILE2.TMP and FILE3.TMP. FILE2.TMP should contain the text shown in Fig. 4.2; FILE3.TMP, the text shown in Fig. 4.3. These two files contain text that we want to preserve. Change the name of the file FILE3.TMP to ASMSUB.LIB with the command

> *REN ASMSUB.LIB=FILE3.TMP*

If CCP responds with the message FILE EXISTS, you will have to invent a name other than ASMSUB.LIB for our *assembly language subroutine library*.

We will now use PIP to copy the subroutines from FILE2.TMP into our library. Append this file with the command

PIP ASMSUB.LIB=ASMSUB.LIB,FILE2.TMP

Use the command

TYPE ASMSUB.LIB

to verify that all routines from both FILE3.TMP and FILE2.TMP are now in ASMSUB.LIB.

Use a directory command in the form

*DIR *.TMP*

to verify that the only file names that satisfy this ambiguous file name are FILE1.TMP and FILE2.TMP. Erase these two files with the command

*ERA *.TMP*

This command will erase, on the current disk, all files whose names end with .TMP.

Rename our library file with the command

REN SUBLIB.ASM=ASMSUB.LIB

Verify an error-free assembler processing of our library with the command

ASM SUBLIB.AZZ

This form of assembler call command causes the assembler to omit creation of .HEX and .PRN files.

Adding a Subroutine to the Library

We are ready now to add a new subroutine to our library. Call the editor with the command

ED SUBLIB.ASM

Bring the first 35 lines of the file into the text buffer with the command

35A

Display 12 lines with the command

12T

If we are positioned where we want to be, then this display will begin with the text lines

;

;   DHB—Display Hex Btye.

```
;        Display two hex digits
;        Entry A = byte to be displayed
;
```

Verify the text pointer location with the command 5T, which should again display these same five comment lines. Put the editor into input-mode with i followed by carriage return. Type in the following text:

```
;
;        DHW—Display Hex Word.
;        Display four hex digits
;        Entry HL = word to be displayed
;
DHW: PUSH H
        MOV A,H      ;Display high byte
        CALL DHB
        POP H
        MOV A,L      ;Display low byte
```

After entering the carriage return that ends the last line of text, get out of input-mode with Control-Z, and then end the edit session with the E command.
Check the new library file for assembly errors with the command

ASM SUBLIB.AZZ

If any assembly errors are indicated, create an assembly listing .PRN file with the command

ASM SUBLIB.AZA

Print out the listing with the command

PIP PRN:=SUBLIB.PRN

Use the editor to correct any errors and then reassemble, repeating these steps until the assembly is error-free. To help find any errors, carefully compare your listing with the assembly listing in Fig. 6.1. The next program we are going to write will use the subroutine library that we have created.

A Program to Count Directory Entries

We will now write a program that will examine the disk directory and count the directory spaces that are occupied. Using the proposed name DIRSIZE, or a name of your choice, call the editor with a command of the form

ED DIRSIZE.ASM

The editor should respond with NEW FILE. Put the editor into input-mode with i followed by carriage return. Type the text shown in Fig. 6.2. Then get out of input-mode with Control-Z, and end the edit session with the E command.

```
                           ;
                           ;            DHW - Display Hex Word.
                           ;            Entry   HL = word to be displayed
                           ;
        0000 E5            DHW:         PUSH H
        0001 7C                         MOV A,H          ;Display high byte
        0002 CD0700                     CALL DHB
        0005 E1                         POP H
        0006 7D                         MOV A,L          ;Display low byte
                           ;
                           ;            DHB - Display Hex Byte.
                           ;            Display two hex digits.
                           ;            Entry   A = byte to be displayed
                           ;
        0007 F5            DHB:         PUSH PSW
        0008 0F0F0F0F                   RRC ! RRC ! RRC ! RRC
        000C CD1000                     CALL DHD         ;display hex digit
        000F F1                         POP PSW
                           ;
                           ;            DHD - Display Hex Digit.
                           ;            Entry   A,low 4 bits = digit
                           ;
        0010 E60F          DHD:         ANI 0FH
        0012 FE0A                       CPI 10
        0014 D21C00                     JNC DHD1         ;If not 0 through 9
                           ;
        0017 C630                       ADI '0'
        0019 C31E00                     JMP DCH
                           ;
        001C C637          DHD1:        ADI 'A'-10       ;Create "A,B,C,D,E, or F"
                           ;
                           ;            DCH - Display one character.
                           ;            Entry   A = ASCII encoded char
                           ;
        001E 5F            DCH:         MOV E,A
        001F 0E02                       MVI C,2
        0021 CD0500                     CALL 5
        0024 C9                         RET
                           ;
                           ;            ALN - Advance to new line.
                           ;            Issue CR,LF
                           ;
        0025 3E0D          ALN:         MVI A,0DH        ;carriage-return
        0027 CD1E00                     CALL DCH
        002A 3E0A                       MVI A,0AH        ;line-feed
        002C CD1E00                     CALL DCH
        002F C9                         RET
                           ;
                           ;            FCC - Filter out Control Codes.
                           ;            Entry   A = ASCII code
                           ;            Exit    B = ASCII graphic char
                           ;                    A = 'up-arrow' if control-code
                           ;                      = blank, if graphic
                           ;
        0030 FE20          FCC:         CPI 20H
        0032 D23B00                     JNC FCC1         ;If not control code
                           ;
                           ;            We have a control-code.
                           ;            Return 'up-arrow' in A; graphic in B.
                           ;
        0035 C640                       ADI 40H
        0037 47                         MOV B,A
        0038 3E5E                       MVI A,5EH        ;up-arrow
        003A C9                         RET
                           ;
                           ;            We have a graphic character.
                           ;            Return blank in A; graphic in B.
                           ;
        003B 47            FCC1:        MOV B,A
        003C 3E20                       MVI A,20H        ;blank
        003E C9                         RET
                           ;
                           ;            MSG - Issue Message to Console.
                           ;            Entry   DE = message address
                           ;
        003F 0E09          MSG:         MVI C,9
```

Fig. 6.1 Assembly listing of subroutine library

```
0041 CD0500              CALL 5
0044 C9                  RET
                ;
                ;       RCC - Read a Console Character.
                ;       Exit    A = character
                ;
0045 0E01       RCC:     MVI C,1
0047 CD0500              CALL 5
004A C9                  RET
```

Fig. 6.1 Assembly listing of subroutine library (Cont.)

Append the subroutine library to the new program with PIP using the command

PIP DIRSIZE.ASM=DIRSIZE.ASM,SUBLIB.ASM

Assemble the new program with the command

ASM DIRSIZE

If there are assembly errors, print out the assembly listing with the command

PIP PRN:=DIRSIZE.PRN

```
;File:  DIRSIZE.ASM
;
;       DIRSIZE - Display directory size.
;       Count the number of occupied slots
;       in the disk directory.
;
        ORG 100H
DRS:    LXI H,0         ;Preset COUNT = 0
        SHLD COUNT
        LXI D,BUFF      ;Set buffer address
        MVI C,1AH
        CALL 5
;
        MVI C,11H       ;Find first occurence
        LXI D,FCB
        CALL 5
        CPI 0FFH
        JZ DRS2         ;If done
;
DRS1:   CALL AEC        ;Advance entry count
        MVI C,12h       ;Find next occurence
        CALL 5
        CPI 0FFH
        JNZ DRS1        ;If not done
;
;       Display the resulting count.
;
DRS2:   CALL ALN        ;CR,LF
        LHLD COUNT
        CALL DHW        ;Display hex word
        LXI D,DRSA      ;"entries used"
        CALL MSG
        JMP 0000
;
;       AEC - Advance Entry Count.
;
AEC:    LHLD COUNT
        INX H
        SHLD COUNT
        RET
;
DRSA:   DB      ' directory entries are currently'
        DB      ' occupied (value in hex).$'
COUNT:  DW      0
FCB:    DB      0,'???????????',0,0,0,0
        DS      20
```

Fig. 6.2 Text for DIRSIZE main program

and carefully compare your listing with the assembly listing in Fig. 6.3. Edit and reassemble until you have an error-free assembly. When the program produces this assembly, create the file DIRSIZE.COM by calling the loader with the command

LOAD DIRSIZE

Execute your new program with the command

DIRSIZE

Your program should respond with a one-line display such as

0019 directory entries are currently occupied (value in hex)

```
                    ;File:   DIRSIZE.ASM
                    ;
                    ;        DIRSIZE - Display directory size.
                    ;        Count the number of occupied slots
                    ;        in the disk directory.
                    ;
0100                         ORG 100H
0100 210000    DRS:          LXI H,0           ;Preset COUNT = 0
0103 227C01                  SHLD COUNT
0106 110002                  LXI D,BUFF        ;Set buffer address
0109 0E1A                    MVI C,1AH
010B CD0500                  CALL 5
                    ;
010E 0E11                    MVI C,11H         ;Find first occurence
0110 117E01                  LXI D,FCB
0113 CD0500                  CALL 5
0116 FEFF                    CPI 0FFH
0118 CA2801                  JZ DRS2           ;If done
                    ;
011B CD3A01    DRS1:         CALL AEC          ;Advance entry count
011E 0E12                    MVI C,12h         ;Find next occurence
0120 CD0500                  CALL 5
0123 FEFF                    CPI 0FFH
0125 C21B01                  JNZ DRS1          ;If not done
                    ;
                    ;        Display the resulting count.
                    ;
0128 CDC701    DRS2:         CALL ALN          ;CR,LF
012B 2A7C01                  LHLD COUNT
012E CDA201                  CALL DHW          ;Display hex word
0131 114201                  LXI D,DRSA        ;"entries used"
0134 CDE101                  CALL MSG
0137 C30000                  JMP 0000
                    ;
                    ;        AEC - Advance Entry Count.
                    ;
013A 2A7C01    AEC:          LHLD COUNT
013D 23                      INX H
013E 227C01                  SHLD COUNT
0141 C9                      RET
                    ;
0142 2064697265 DRSA:  DB    ' directory entries are currently'
0162 206F636375        DB    ' occupied (value in hex).$'
017C 0000      COUNT:  DW    0
017E 003F3F3F3F FCB:   DB    0,'???????????',0,0,0,0
018E                   DS    20
                    ;
                    ;        DHW - Display Hex Word.
                    ;        Entry   HL = word to be displayed
                    ;
01A2 E5        DHW:          PUSH H
01A3 7C                      MOV A,H            ;Display high byte
01A4 CDA901                  CALL DHB
01A7 E1                      POP H
01A8 7D                      MOV A,L            ;Display low byte
                    ;
                    ;        DHB - Display Hex Byte.
```

Fig. 6.3 Assembly listing of DIRSIZE

```
                       ;            Display two hex digits.
                       ;            Entry   A = byte to be displayed
                       ;
01A9 F5                DHB:         PUSH PSW
01AA 0F0F0F0F                       RRC ! RRC ! RRC ! RRC
01AE CDB201                         CALL DHD          ;display hex digit
01B1 F1                             POP PSW
                       ;
                       ;            DHD - Display Hex Digit.
                       ;            Entry   A,low 4 bits = digit
                       ;
01B2 E60F              DHD:         ANI 0FH
01B4 FE0A                           CPI 10
01B6 D2BE01                         JNC DHD1          ;If not 0 through 9
                       ;
01B9 C630                           ADI '0'
01BB C3C001                         JMP DCH
                       ;
01BE C637              DHD1:        ADI 'A'-10        ;Create "A,B,C,D,E, or F"
                       ;
                       ;            DCH - Display one character.
                       ;            Entry   A = ASCII encoded char
                       ;
01C0 5F                DCH:         MOV E,A
01C1 0E02                           MVI C,2
01C3 CD0500                         CALL 5
01C6 C9                             RET
                       ;
                       ;            ALN - Advance to new line.
                       ;            Issue CR,LF
                       ;
01C7 3E0D              ALN:         MVI A,0DH         ;carriage-return
01C9 CDC001                         CALL DCH
01CC 3E0A                           MVI A,0AH         ;line-feed
01CE CDC001                         CALL DCH
01D1 C9                             RET
                       ;
                       ;            FCC - Filter out Control Codes.
                       ;            Entry   A = ASCII code
                       ;            Exit    B = ASCII graphic char
                       ;                    A = 'up-arrow' if control-code
                       ;                      = blank, if graphic
                       ;
01D2 FE20              FCC:         CPI 20H
01D4 D2DD01                         JNC FCC1          ;If not control code
                       ;
                       ;            We have a control-code.
                       ;            Return 'up-arrow' in A; graphic in B.
                       ;
01D7 C640                           ADI 40H
01D9 47                             MOV B,A
01DA 3E5E                           MVI A,5EH         ;up-arrow
01DC C9                             RET
                       ;
                       ;            We have a graphic character.
                       ;            Return blank in A; graphic in B.
                       ;
01DD 47                FCC1:        MOV B,A
01DE 3E20                           MVI A,20H         ;blank
01E0 C9                             RET
                       ;
                       ;            MSG - Issue Message to Console.
                       ;            Entry   DE = message address
                       ;
01E1 0E09              MSG:         MVI C,9
01E3 CD0500                         CALL 5
01E6 C9                             RET
                       ;
                       ;            RCC - Read a Console Character.
                       ;            Exit    A = character
                       ;
01E7 0E01              RCC:         MVI C,1
01E9 CD0500                         CALL 5
01EC C9                             RET
                       ;
0200                                ORG      200H
0200 =                 BUFF         EQU      $
```

Fig. 6.3 Assembly listing of DIRSIZE (Cont.)

This program uses the CP/M's *search-for-next-occurrence function* to search the directory for all occurrences of the file named ????????.???. Since this file name matches every name in the directory, the net result of counting all of its occurrences is a count of all of the directory spaces that are occupied.

File Attributes

The number of occupied directory spaces can be greater than the number of files displayed by the DIR command. The DIR command ignores system files and displays only the first *extent* of large files that occupy more than one directory space. Using the terminology from the Digital Research "CP/M 2.2 Interface Guide," the eight characters of the file name are designated f1 through f8, and the three characters of the file type are designated t1 through t3, with the arrangement

f1 f2 f3 f4 f5 f6 f7 f8 . t1 t2 t3

Each character in the file name and file type is an ASCII character stored in the low-order seven bits of the eight-bit byte. When BDOS examines a file name, it ignores the high-order bit of each ASCII byte. These high-order bits are thus made available as *flags* that can be used to assign *attributes* to the file. For example, if the high-order bit t1, called t1', is set to 1, then BDOS will not write into the file, and the file is said to have been marked "Read-Only." If the high-order bit t2, called t2', is set to 1, then the file name won't appear in the DIR display created by CCP, and the file is said to be a *system file*. The command

STAT *.*

displays system files with their file names in parentheses.

Examining the Directory

When DIRSIZE returns control to CCP, save the memory image left behind by DIRSIZE, using the command

SAVE 2 IMAGE.COM

Load this image back into memory with DDT, using the command

DDT IMAGE.COM

Examine memory at location 0200 with the DDT command

D200,27F

These 128 bytes contain an image of one CP/M sector of the *disk file directory*. There is room in this sector for four directory entries, each of which occupies 32 bytes, or two lines of the display. The 32 bytes of each directory entry are numbered 00 through 1F hex. Any directory entry that has the hex value E5 in byte 00 is known as an *erased entry*.

Counting Entries for a Specific File

Copy the source code for DIRSIZE into a file named DIRIMAGE.ASM by using the command

PIP DIRIMAGE.ASM=DIRSIZE.ASM

Call the editor with the command

ED DIRIMAGE.ASM

Now bring in the first 60 lines of the file with the command

60A

and change the name in the first line of the file from DIRSIZE to DIRIMAGE with the command

SSIZE↑ZIMAGE↑Z0LT

Delete the label FCB: with the command

SFCB:↑Z↑Z0LT

Go into input-mode with i followed by carriage return, and type the new line of text

FCB EQU 5CH ;Get filename from CCP

followed by carriage return. Get out of input-mode with Control-Z, and then end the edit session with the E command.

Assemble DIRIMAGE with the command

ASM DIRIMAGE

If there are assembly errors, print out the assembly listing with the command

PIP PRN:=DIRIMAGE.PRN

and carefully examine your source text. Edit and reassemble until you have an error-free assembly. Then create the command file DIRIMAGE.COM with the command

LOAD DIRIMAGE

Testing the Program with PIP.COM

Call the new program with the command

DIRIMAGE PIP.COM

The program will count and display the number of occurrences of the file name PIP.COM. Save the memory image left by DIRIMAGE with the command

SAVE 2 IMAGE.COM

Reload the memory image under DDT with the command

    DDT IMAGE.COM

and display memory at location 0200 with the DDT command

    D200,27F

You should find that there is indeed a directory sector image in the buffer at location 0200, but it may not contain the directory entry for PIP.COM. If you are interested in learning assembly language programming, study the program to see if you can determine the correction needed before reading further.

The problem appears to be that the program is always leaving us with only the last sector of the directory in the buffer. We can correct this situation by making the program advance the buffer location for each directory sector.

Get out of DDT and call the editor with the command

    ED DIRIMAGE.ASM

Bring in 60 lines with 60A, and find the first CALL with the command

    FCALL↑Z0LT

Go to the next line with carriage return, and then insert the two new text lines

    LXI H,FCB+0CH   ;Set ambiguous extent
    MVI M,'?'

Find the line beginning DRS1: with the command

    FDRS1:↑Z0LT

Move the text pointer to the next line by pressing carriage return. Go into input-mode with i followed by carriage return, and then type the following additional instructions:

    LHLD DMA   ;Advance buffer address
    LXI D,128
    DAD D
    SHLD DMA
    XCHG
    MVI C,1AH
    CALL 5

ending each line with carriage return. Get out of input-mode with Control-Z, and review the modifications with −12L23T.

Write out the current 60 lines to the disk with the command

    #W

Bring in the next 60 lines of text with the command

> *60A*

and write these 60 lines out without modification with the command

> *#W*

Bring in the remaining text with the command

> *60A*

Display the current text buffer contents with the command

> *#T*

There should now be only about a dozen lines in the buffer. In the next-to-last line of the program, change 200H to 300H with the command

> *S200H↑Z300H↑Z0LT*

Then insert a new line of text in front of this ORG line by entering input-mode with i followed by carriage return.
Type in the line

> *DMA: DW BUFF*

followed by carriage return. Get out of input-mode with Control-Z, and then end the edit session with the E command.
Reassemble DIRIMAGE with the command

> *ASM DIRIMAGE*

Create the command file with

> *LOAD DIRIMAGE*

Compare your assembly listing of the final program with the listing in Fig. 6.4. Call the program with the command

> *DIRIMAGE PIP.COM*

Save the memory image left behind by DIRIMAGE with the command

> *SAVE 3 IMAGE.COM*

Load the memory image under DDT with the command

> *DDT IMAGE.COM*

Display memory at location 0300 with the DDT command

> *D300,37F*

```
                         ;File:   DIRIMAGE.ASM
                         ;
                         ;         DIRIMAGE - Count the number of
                         ;         directory spaces occupied by a
                         ;         named file.
                         ;
    0100                          ORG  100H
    0100  210000    DRS:          LXI  H,0          ;Preset COUNT = 0
    0103  229101                  SHLD COUNT
    0106  110003                  LXI  D,BUFF       ;Set buffer address
    0109  0E1A                    MVI  C,1AH
    010B  CD0500                  CALL 5
    010E  216800                  LXI  H,FCB+0CH    ;Set ambiguous extent
    0111  363F                    MVI  M,'?'
                         ;
    0113  0E11                    MVI  C,11H        ;Find first occurence
    0115  115C00                  LXI  D,FCB
    0118  CD0500                  CALL 5
    011B  FEFF                    CPI  0FFH
    011D  CA3D01                  JZ   DRS2         ;If done
                         ;
    0120  CD4F01    DRS1:         CALL AEC          ;Advance entry count
    0123  2A0202                  LHLD DMA          ;Advance buffer address
    0126  118000                  LXI  D,128
    0129  19                      DAD  D
    012A  220202                  SHLD DMA
    012D  EB                      XCHG
    012E  0E1A                    MVI  C,1AH
    0130  CD0500                  CALL 5
    0133  0E12                    MVI  C,12h        ;Find next occurence
    0135  CD0500                  CALL 5
    0138  FEFF                    CPI  0FFH
    013A  C22001                  JNZ  DRS1         ;If not done
                         ;
                         ;         Display the resulting count.
                         ;
    013D  CDDC01    DRS2:         CALL ALN          ;CR,LF
    0140  2A9101                  LHLD COUNT
    0143  CDB701                  CALL DHW          ;Display hex word
    0146  115701                  LXI  D,DRSA       ;"entries used"
    0149  CDF601                  CALL MSG
    014C  C30000                  JMP  0000
                         ;
                         ;         AEC - Advance Entry Count.
                         ;
    014F  2A9101    AEC:          LHLD COUNT
    0152  23                      INX  H
    0153  229101                  SHLD COUNT
    0156  C9                      RET
                         ;
    0157  2064697265DRSA:         DB   ' directory entries are currently'
    0177  206F636375              DB   ' occupied (value in hex).$'
    0191  0000      COUNT:        DW   0
    005C  =         FCB           EQU  5CH          ;Get filename from CCP
    0193  003F3F3F3F              DB   0,'???????????',0,0,0,0
    01A3                          DS   20
                         ;
                         ;         DHW - Display Hex Word.
                         ;         Entry   HL = word to be displayed
                         ;
    01B7  E5        DHW:          PUSH H
    01B8  7C                      MOV  A,H          ;Display high byte
    01B9  CDBE01                  CALL DHB
    01BC  E1                      POP  H
    01BD  7D                      MOV  A,L          ;Display low byte
                         ;
                         ;         DHB - Display Hex Byte.
                         ;         Display two hex digits.
                         ;         Entry   A = byte to be displayed
                         ;
    01BE  F5        DHB:          PUSH PSW
    01BF  0F0F0F0F               RRC ! RRC ! RRC ! RRC
    01C3  CDC701                  CALL DHD          ;display hex digit
```

Fig. 6.4 *Assembly listing of DIRIMAGE*

```
01C6 F1                      POP PSW
                    ;
                    ;        DHD - Display Hex Digit.
                    ;        Entry   A,low 4 bits = digit
                    ;
01C7 E60F           DHD:     ANI 0FH
01C9 FE0A                    CPI 10
01CB D2D301                  JNC DHD1          ;If not 0 through 9
                    ;
01CE C630                    ADI '0'
01D0 C3D501                  JMP DCH
                    ;
01D3 C637           DHD1:    ADI 'A'-10        ;Create "A,B,C,D,E, or F"
                    ;
                    ;        DCH - Display one character.
                    ;        Entry   A = ASCII encoded char
                    ;
01D5 5F             DCH:     MOV E,A
01D6 0E02                    MVI C,2
01D8 CD0500                  CALL 5
01DB C9                      RET
                    ;
                    ;        ALN - Advance to new line.
                    ;        Issue CR,LF
                    ;
01DC 3E0D           ALN:     MVI A,0DH         ;carriage-return
01DE CDD501                  CALL DCH
01E1 3E0A                    MVI A,0AH         ;line-feed
01E3 CDD501                  CALL DCH
01E6 C9                      RET
                    ;
                    ;        FCC - Filter out Control Codes.
                    ;        Entry   A = ASCII code
                    ;        Exit    B = ASCII graphic char
                    ;                A = 'up-arrow' if control-code
                    ;                  = blank, if graphic
                    ;
01E7 FE20           FCC:     CPI 20H
01E9 D2F201                  JNC FCC1          ;If not control code
                    ;
                    ;        We have a control-code.
                    ;        Return 'up-arrow' in A; graphic in B.
                    ;
01EC C640                    ADI 40H
01EE 47                      MOV B,A
01EF 3E5E                    MVI A,5EH         ;up-arrow
01F1 C9                      RET
                    ;
                    ;        We have a graphic character.
                    ;        Return blank in A; graphic in B.
                    ;
01F2 47             FCC1:    MOV B,A
01F3 3E20                    MVI A,20H         ;blank
01F5 C9                      RET
                    ;
                    ;        MSG - Issue Message to Console.
                    ;        Entry   DE = message address
                    ;
01F6 0E09           MSG:     MVI C,9
01F8 CD0500                  CALL 5
01FB C9                      RET
                    ;
                    ;        RCC - Read a Console Character.
                    ;        Exit   A = character
                    ;
01FC 0E01           RCC:     MVI C,1
01FE CD0500                  CALL 5
0201 C9                      RET
                    ;
0202 0003           DMA:     DW      BUFF
0300                         ORG     300H
0300 =              BUFF     EQU     $
```

Fig. 6.4 Assembly listing of DIRIMAGE (Cont.)

This copy of a directory sector should contain an image of the directory entry for the file PIP.COM

The Directory Entry

A CP/M directory entry always contains 32 bytes. The bytes of each directory entry are numbered in hex from 00 through 1F. If the entry is empty, that is, if the file has been erased, then the first byte of the entry, byte 00, will contain the hex value E5. If the first byte contains something other than E5, then the entry is active, that is, it is associated with an existing file. Under CP/M 1.4, the only thing that will appear in byte 00 of an entry is E5 or 00. Under CP/M 2.2, however, you may find numbers other than 00 in byte 00 of an active entry. For example, an entry with 05 in byte 00 is an active entry belonging to USER 5.

Bytes 01 through 08 contain the file name. Bytes 09 through 0B contain the file type. Byte 0C, called the *extent byte*, is used to number the additional directory entries needed by larger files. Byte 0D is unused. Byte 0E, called S2, is unused in CP/M 1.4 but contains four bits of the nine-bit extent count used by CP/M 2.2. Byte 0F, called the *record count*, gives the number of CP/M records in the current extent.

File Extents

On any CP/M standard 8-inch single-density disk, the terms *extent* and *directory entry* are synonymous. On higher capacity disks, a single directory entry can contain more than one *logical* extent. The generalized *extent* of CP/M 2.2 is discussed in greater detail in Appendix C.

Directory Structure

Bytes 10 through 1F contain the names of the *blocks* of disk space reserved for this file. Bytes 10 through 1F are said to be an entry in the *Record Block Table*, or RBT. Bytes 00 through 0F of the directory entry are said to be an entry in the *File Name Table*, or FNT. The disk directory is seen to be an interlaced merger of these two tables that allows entries in the FNT to be associated with entries in the RBT. Processing of the RBT, its creation, and especially its updating are central topics of Chaps. 10 and 11.

Exercise

The subroutine named FCC is present but not used in DIRSIZE and also in DIRIMAGE. Counting the .ASM and .PRN files, we have four unneeded images of this text on the disk. How much disk space would be saved if we deleted the subroutine FCC in these files?

Answer
Use the command

 STAT DIR *.*

to display the sizes of all these files. You should find, for example, that the file DIRSIZE.ASM occupies 18 CP/M records. On a CP/M standard 8-inch single-density disk, where the reservation block size is eight CP/M records, this file will occupy 2.25 reservation blocks and therefore must have three blocks reserved for it. If deleting FCC shrinks the file by 0.25 blocks, or two CP/M records, or 256 bytes, then one block of disk space will be saved. On a high-capacity disk with 32 CP/M records per reservation block, however, no disk space would be saved.

Summary

In this chapter we have developed one program that counts all the occupied spaces in the disk directory and a second program that counts the directory spaces occupied by a specific file. These exercises have provided an introduction to the CP/M search-for-file functions and have given us the opportunity to examine details of the CP/M disk directory.

CHAPTER 7

Your System
Memory Map

IN THIS CHAPTER our objective is to develop an accurate memory map of your CP/M system.

Memory Map Program

First select a name such as MEMMAP.ASM for the program that we are going to write. Use the command

DIR MEMMAP.*

to verify availability of this file name. Should it be already in use, you'll have to invent another. The "primary" name to the left of the period can contain up to eight letters; the "secondary" name to the right of the period must be ASM. If you invent a name other than MEMMAP, substitute your invented name wherever MEMMAP appears hereafter.

Call the editor with the command

ED MEMMAP.ASM

The editor, which will be loaded and started by CCP, will issue the message NEW FILE and then display the command-mode prompt(*). Put the editor into input-mode with i followed by carriage return, and type the program text shown in Fig. 7.1. After typing this text, get out of input-mode with Control-Z, and end the edit session with the E command.

Call PIP to append our subroutine library to the new program file, using the command

PIP MEMMAP.ASM=MEMMAP.ASM,SUBLIB.ASM

```
        ;File:   MEMMAP.ASM
        ;
        ;        Display CP/M memory locations.
        ;
                ORG 100H
                MVI C,12        ;Check 1.4 or 2.2
                CALL 5
                MOV A,L
                ORA A
                LXI H,3328-6    ;Length of 1.4 BDOS
                JZ MMP1         ;If CP/M version 1.4
        ;
                LXI H,3584-6    ;Length of 2.2 BDOS
                MVI A,'2'       ;Change message
                STA MMPK
                STA MMPK+2
MMP1:           SHLD MMPA
        ;
                LHLD 6          ;Get BDOS entry address
                SHLD BDOSE
                LXI B,-806H     ;Calculate CCP fwa
                DAD B
                SHLD CCPFWA
        ;
                DCX H           ;Calculate TPA lwa
                SHLD TPALWA
                INX H
        ;
                LXI B,800H      ;Calculate BDOS fwa
                DAD B
                SHLD BDFWA
                LXI B,6         ;Calculate BDOS entry address
                DAD B
                SHLD BDOSE
        ;
                LXI B,0         ;Calculate CBIOS fwa
MMPA            EQU $-2
                DAD B
                SHLD CBFWA
        ;
                LXI B,3         ;Calculate CBIOS "warmboot" entry address
                DAD B
                SHLD WRMBT
        ;
        ;        Display memory locations.
        ;
                LXI D,MMPB      ;Display a line of dashes "-----------"
                CALL MSG
                LXI D,MMPJ      ;Display system version number
                CALL MSG
                LXI D,MMPC      ;"warmboot" etc
                CALL MSG
        ;
                LXI H,0         ;Display TPA lwa
TPALWA          EQU $-2
                CALL DHW
                LXI D,MMPD
                CALL MSG
        ;
                LXI H,0         ;Display CCP fwa
CCPFWA          EQU $-2
                CALL DHW
                LXI D,MMPE
                CALL MSG
        ;
                LXI H,0         ;Display BDOS fwa
BDFWA           EQU $-2
                CALL DHW
                LXI D,MMPF
                CALL MSG
        ;
                LXI H,0         ;Display BDOS entry address
BDOSE           EQU $-2
                CALL DHW
                LXI D,MMPG
```

Fig. 7.1 Text for MEMMAP

```
        CALL MSG
;
        LXI H,0          ;Display CBIOS fwa
CBFWA   EQU $-2
        CALL DHW
        LXI D,MMPH
        CALL MSG
;
        LXI H,0          ;Display CBIOS warmboot entry location
WRMBT   EQU $-2
        CALL DHW
        LXI D,MMPI
        CALL MSG
;
        LXI D,MMPB       ;Display a line of dashes "-------"
        CALL MSG
        JMP 0000
;
CR      EQU 0DH
LF      EQU 0AH
;
MMPB:   DB      CR,LF,'-------------------------------------'
        DB      CR,LF,'$'
MMPC:   DB      '0000 "warmboot" vector',CR,LF
        DB      '0005 BDOS vector',CR,LF
        DB      '005C default file control block (FCB)',CR,LF
        DB      '0080 CP/M record buffer',CR,LF
        DB      '0100 first word address (fwa) of user area',CR,LF,'$'
MMPD:   DB      ' last word address (lwa) of user area',CR,LF,'$'
MMPE:   DB      ' CCP fwa',CR,LF,'$'
MMPF:   DB      ' BDOS fwa',CR,LF,'$'
MMPG:   DB      ' BDOS entry point',CR,LF,'$'
MMPH:   DB      ' CBIOS fwa',CR,LF,'$'
MMPI:   DB      ' CBIOS warmboot entry point',CR,LF,'$'
MMPJ:   DB      'System:  CP/M Version '
MMPK:   DB      '1.4',CR,LF,'$'
```

Fig. 7.1 *Text for MEMMAP (Cont.)*

Assemble the new program with the command

ASM MEMMAP

If there are any assembly errors, print out the assembly listing with the command

PIP PRN:=MEMMAP.PRN

Alternatively, you can display the assembly listing on the screen with the command

TYPE MEMMAP.PRN

stopping and starting scrolling of the display with Control-S. Or, as another alternative, you can display the assembly listing on the screen and simultaneously print a copy of it by putting CP/M into console-print mode with Control-P prior to using the TYPE command. As yet another alternative, you can load the assembly listing file under the editor in order to display selected portions of the file that are of interest.

Carefully compare your assembly listing with the assembly listing of MEMMAP in Fig. 7.2. Then use the editor to make any needed modifications of the source file MEMMAP.ASM. Suppose, for example, that the text line that should have read

MMPH: DB ' CBIOS fwa',CR,LF,'$'

```
                        ;File:   MEMMAP.ASM
                        ;
                        ;       Display CP/M memory locations.
                        ;
0100                            ORG    100H
0100 0E0C                       MVI    C,12         ;Check 1.4 or 2.2
0102 CD0500                     CALL   5
0105 7D                         MOV    A,L
0106 B7                         ORA    A
0107 21FA0C                     LXI    H,3328-6     ;Length of 1.4 BDOS
010A CA1801                     JZ     MMP1         ;If CP/M version 1.4
                        ;
010D 21FA0D                     LXI    H,3584-6     ;Length of 2.2 BDOS
0110 3E32                       MVI    A,'2'        ;Change message
0112 320303                     STA    MMPK
0115 320503                     STA    MMPK+2
0118 223C01      MMP1:          SHLD   MMPA
                        ;
011B 2A0600                     LHLD   6            ;Get BDOS entry address
011E 228001                     SHLD   BDOSE
0121 01FAF7                     LXI    B,-806H      ;Calculate CCP fwa
0124 09                         DAD    B
0125 226801                     SHLD   CCPFWA
                        ;
0128 2B                         DCX    H            ;Calculate TPA lwa
0129 225C01                     SHLD   TPALWA
012C 23                         INX    H
                        ;
012D 010008                     LXI    B,800H       ;Calculate BDOS fwa
0130 09                         DAD    B
0131 227401                     SHLD   BDFWA
0134 010600                     LXI    B,6          ;Calculate BDOS entry address
0137 09                         DAD    B
0138 228001                     SHLD   BDOSE
                        ;
013B 010000                     LXI    B,0          ;Calculate CBIOS fwa
013C =           MMPA           EQU    $-2
013E 09                         DAD    B
013F 228C01                     SHLD   CBFWA
                        ;
0142 010300                     LXI    B,3          ;Calculate CBIOS "warmboot" entry address
0145 09                         DAD    B
0146 229801                     SHLD   WRMBT
                        ;
                        ;       Display memory locations.
0149 11AC01                     LXI    D,MMPB       ;Display a line of dashes "----------"
014C CD4803                     CALL   MSG
014F 11ED02                     LXI    D,MMPJ       ;Display system version number
0152 CD4803                     CALL   MSG
0155 11D801                     LXI    D,MMPC       ;"warmboot" etc
0158 CD4803                     CALL   MSG
                        ;
015B 210000                     LXI    H,0          ;Display TPA lwa
015C =           TPALWA         EQU    $-2
015E CD0903                     CALL   DHW
0161 116F02                     LXI    D,MMPD
0164 CD4803                     CALL   MSG
                        ;
0167 210000                     LXI    H,0          ;Display CCP fwa
0168 =           CCPFWA         EQU    $-2
016A CD0903                     CALL   DHW
016D 119702                     LXI    D,MMPE
0170 CD4803                     CALL   MSG
                        ;
0173 210000                     LXI    H,0          ;Display BDOS fwa
0174 =           BDFWA          EQU    $-2
0176 CD0903                     CALL   DHW
0179 11A202                     LXI    D,MMPF
017C CD4803                     CALL   MSG
                        ;
017F 210000                     LXI    H,0          ;Display BDOS entry address
0180 =           BDOSE          EQU    $-2
0182 CD0903                     CALL   DHW
0185 11AE02                     LXI    D,MMPG
0188 CD4803                     CALL   MSG
```

Fig. 7.2 *Assembly listing of MEMMAP*

```
                      ;
018B 210000                   LXI  H,0              ;Display CBIOS fwa
018C =        CBFWA    EQU  $-2
018E CD0903                   CALL DHW
0191 11C202                   LXI  D,MMPH
0194 CD4803                   CALL MSG
                      ;
0197 210000                   LXI  H,0              ;Display CBIOS warmboot entry location
0198 =        WRMBT    EQU  $-2
019A CD0903                   CALL DHW
019D 11CF02                   LXI  D,MMPI
01A0 CD4803                   CALL MSG
                      ;
01A3 11AC01                   LXI  D,MMPB           ;Display a line of dashes "-------"
01A6 CD4803                   CALL MSG
01A9 C30000                   JMP  0000
                      ;
000D =        CR       EQU  0DH
000A =        LF       EQU  0AH
                      ;
01AC 0D0A2D2D2DMMPB:  DB       CR,LF,'-------------------------------------'
01D5 0D0A24           DB       CR,LF,'$'
01D8 3030303020MMPC:  DB       '0000 "warmboot" vector',CR,LF
01F0 3030303520       DB       '0005 BDOS vector',CR,LF
0202 3030354320       DB       '005C default file control block (FCB)',CR,LF
0229 3030383020       DB       '0080 CP/M record buffer',CR,LF
0242 3031303020       DB       '0100 first word address (fwa) of user area',CR,LF,'$'
026F 206C617374MMPD:  DB       ' last word address (lwa) of user area',CR,LF,'$'
0297 2043435020MMPE:  DB       ' CCP fwa',CR,LF,'$'
02A2 2042444F53MMPF:  DB       ' BDOS fwa',CR,LF,'$'
02AE 2042444F53MMPG:  DB       ' BDOS entry point',CR,LF,'$'
02C2 204342494FMMPH:  DB       ' CBIOS fwa',CR,LF,'$'
02CF 204342494FMMPI:  DB       ' CBIOS warmboot entry point',CR,LF,'$'
02ED 5379737465MMPJ:  DB       'System: CP/M Version '
0303 312E340D0AMMPK:  DB       '1.4',CR,LF,'$'
                      ;
                      ;       DHW - Display Hex Word.
                      ;       Entry   HL = word to be displayed
                      ;
0309 E5       DHW:     PUSH H
030A 7C                MOV  A,H              ;Display high byte
030B CD1003            CALL DHB
030E E1                POP  H
030F 7D                MOV  A,L              ;Display low byte
                      ;
                      ;       DHB - Display Hex Byte.
                      ;       Display two hex digits.
                      ;       Entry   A = byte to be displayed
                      ;
0310 F5       DHB:     PUSH PSW
0311 0F0F0F0F          RRC ! RRC ! RRC ! RRC
0315 CD1903            CALL DHD              ;display hex digit
0318 F1                POP  PSW
                      ;
                      ;       DHD - Display Hex Digit.
                      ;       Entry   A,low 4 bits = digit
                      ;
0319 E60F     DHD:     ANI  0FH
031B FE0A              CPI  10
031D D22503            JNC  DHD1             ;If not 0 through 9
                      ;
0320 C630              ADI  '0'
0322 C32703            JMP  DCH
                      ;
0325 C637     DHD1:    ADI  'A'-10           ;Create "A,B,C,D,E, or F"
                      ;
                      ;       DCH - Display one character.
                      ;       Entry   A = ASCII encoded char
                      ;
0327 5F       DCH:     MOV  E,A
0328 0E02              MVI  C,2
032A CD0500            CALL 5
032D C9                RET
                      ;
                      ;       ALN - Advance to new line.
                      ;       Issue CR,LF
```

Fig. 7.2 *Assembly listing of MEMMAP (Cont.)*

```
                         ;
032E 3E0D      ALN:      MVI A,0DH        ;carriage-return
0330 CD2703              CALL DCH
0333 3E0A               MVI A,0AH        ;line-feed
0335 CD2703              CALL DCH
0338 C9                 RET
                         ;
                         ;      FCC - Filter out Control Codes.
                         ;      Entry   A = ASCII code
                         ;      Exit    B = ASCII graphic char
                         ;              A = 'up-arrow' if control-code
                         ;                = blank, if graphic
                         ;
0339 FE20      FCC:      CPI 20H
033B D24403              JNC FCC1         ;If not control code
                         ;
                         ;      We have a control-code.
                         ;      Return 'up-arrow' in A; graphic in B.
                         ;
033E C640               ADI 40H
0340 47                 MOV B,A
0341 3E5E               MVI A,5EH        ;up-arrow
0343 C9                 RET
                         ;
                         ;      We have a graphic character.
                         ;      Return blank in A; graphic in B.
                         ;
0344 47        FCC1:     MOV B,A
0345 3E20               MVI A,20H        ;blank
0347 C9                 RET
                         ;
                         ;      MSG - Issue Message to Console.
                         ;      Entry   DE = message address
                         ;
0348 0E09      MSG:      MVI C,9
034A CD0500              CALL 5
034D C9                 RET
                         ;
                         ;      RCC - Read a Console Character.
                         ;      Exit    A = character
                         ;
034E 0E01      RCC:      MVI C,1
0350 CD0500              CALL 5
0353 C9                 RET
```

Fig. 7.2 *Assembly listing of MEMMAP (Cont.)*

is missing an apostrophe so that it actually reads

MMPH: DB ' CBIOS fwa',CR,LF,$'

Since this omission is an error to the assembler, it will flag the line with the letter O in the assembly listing, meaning "operand error." To correct this error in the source file, call the editor with the command

ED MEMMAP.ASM

Bring the entire file into the text buffer with the #A command followed by carriage return. Move the text pointer directly to the line that is to be corrected by using the find command in the form

FMMPH:↑Z0LT

When the editor displays the line beginning with the label MMPH:, use a substitute command in the form

S$↑Z'$↑Z0LT

to insert the required apostrophe. End the edit session with the E command. Reassemble the program with the command

ASM MEMMAP

Edit and reassemble until you have an error-free assembly. Then create the command file MEMMAP.COM by calling the loader with the command

LOAD MEMMAP

Testing MEMMAP under DDT

We will test the program under controlled conditions by first loading it under DDT with the command

DDT MEMMAP.COM

Use the DDT list command in form

L100,104

and verify that the program begins with

0100   MVI C,0C
0102   CALL 0005

Use the list command L1A9,1AB to verify that the program ends with

01A9 JMP 0000

Use the DDT X command to verify that the program counter is set to 0100. Put CP/M into console-print mode with Control-P, and then run the program by typing

G

followed by carriage return. About a dozen lines should be printed and displayed, and then control should return to CCP. The result created should be similar to that in Fig. 7.3.

```
------------------------------------------
System:  CP/M Version 2.2
0000 "warmboot" vector
0005 BDOS vector
005C default file control block (FCB)
0080 CP/M record buffer
0100 first word address (fwa) of user area
DBFF last word address (lwa) of user area
DC00 CCP fwa
E400 BDOS fwa
E406 BDOS entry point
F200 CBIOS fwa
F203 CBIOS warmboot entry point
------------------------------------------
```

Fig. 7.3 *Example of MEMMAP display*

Now with CP/M still in console-print mode, call the program directly with the command

MEMMAP

Again, you should get about a dozen lines printed and displayed. Compare the results of this direct call to MEMMAP with the results obtained with MEMMAP running under DDT. You should find that the results differ.

MEMMAP Results (the "Vector at 0005")

The first five hex values displayed by MEMMAP will always agree because these are CP/M fixed values that we typed into MEMMAP when we created the file MEMMAP.ASM, but the remaining six values are calculated by MEMMAP. All six of these values depend on the contents of memory location 0006 at the time that MEMMAP executes.

The word at location 0006 is the operand of the JMP instruction at location 0005. MEMMAP displays the value obtained from location 0006 in the display line labeled "BDOS entry point."

The JMP instruction at location 0005 serves two purposes. First, it provides, in a fixed location, linkage to the CP/M system manager, BDOS. Second, it defines the upper limit of user-alterable memory for all user programs. A standard CP/M user program, such as ED, is permitted to use memory from location 0100 up to but not through the location pointed to by the "vector at 0005." This second use for the vector at 0005 explains the difference between the results displayed when MEMMAP is called directly and those displayed when MEMMAP is executed under DDT. DDT changes the vector at 0005 in order to protect itself from being overwritten. Print file spooling programs that load into the area just below CCP will protect themselves in the same manner. To obtain an accurate report from MEMMAP, call it directly before any print file spool utility has been loaded into the system.

Converting a .PRN File to an .ASM File

Call the editor with the command

ED MEMMAP.PRN

and then bring in the entire assembly listing with the #A command. Display the listing with the #T command. Use the command 2T to verify that there are two blank lines at the beginning of the file. If there are, delete them with the 2K command. Use the command

M16D0LTL

to remove the machine code text from each line. When the operation is complete, press Delete twice. Use the B command to move the text pointer back to the beginning of the file. Use the #T command to display the result. You should find that you have converted the assembly listing file back into an assembly language source text file. This operation permits an assembly listing file to act as back-up for an assembly source file.

Exercise

Use the memory addresses obtained from MEMMAP to draw an accurate memory map of your CP/M system. Start with location 0000 at the top of the page, or at the bottom of the page if you prefer, since it is immaterial whether your memory map is drawn top-down or bottom-up. The important thing is to draw the map and thus form a clear mental impression of the actual arrangement of the CP/M resident in your computer.

Summary

In this chapter we've developed a program that displays the actual memory map of your CP/M system. Exercises using this program have provided an introduction to the BDOS vector at memory location 0005. The vector at 0005 provides in a fixed location the linkage between user programs and the CP/M system manager, and it also defines the upper limit of user available memory.

8

Patching a Program

*I*N THIS CHAPTER, after a brief lexicographical digression, we will use DDT to modify the machine code of a program directly. To "patch" a program means to change the machine code program without going through the usual program modification procedure. The usual procedure is to edit the source program and reassemble it to obtain the new machine code program. Patching is a direct operation on machine code.

The program we'll modify is the program named HELLO developed in Chap. 3. This exercise provides an introduction to the *reservation block* that is fundamental to CP/M's disk allocation scheme.

Reviewing HELLO.PRN

Find your hardcopy listing of HELLO or create a new listing with the command

PIP PRN:=HELLO.PRN

Compare your listing with the assembly listing in Fig. 3.4 to verify that you are looking at the same program.

Near the end of the listing, find the assembly language instruction JMP 0000. The assembler has translated this symbolic language instruction into the machine language instruction

C3 00 00

and, as indicated in the listing, the assembler anticipates that the loader will place this machine code into memory locations 012A, 012B, and 012C. The byte C3 will be loaded into location 012A, the byte 00 into location 012B, and the second byte 00 into location 012C. The general machine code form of this *unconditional jump* instruction is

      C3 yy xx

When executed, this instruction will load the 16-bit address xxyy into the program counter. The byte C3 is called the *operation code*, or *op-code*. This operation code tells the 8080 to load the program counter unconditionally from the next two bytes. The two bytes following the op-code are called the *operand*. This op-code has a 16-bit operand, requiring two eight-bit bytes. The 8080 requires the low-order eight bits of the operand to appear in the byte immediately following the op-code. *Low-order* means *right-most*; for example, in the decimal number 85, the 5 is the low-order digit. In the binary number 1000 0011 0110 0010, the low-order bit is 0, the low-order hex digit is 2, and the low-order byte is 62. The high-order bit is 1, the high-order hex digit is 8, and the high-order byte is 83. The full 16-bit word, expressed in hex, is 8362. An instruction JMP 8362 would appear in machine code as C3 62 83.

The term *word* may be used to refer to one or more bytes. For example, some larger machines are said to have 32-bit words. In this book, the term *word* always indicates 16 bits, or two bytes. Since the 8080 uses 16-bit memory addresses, one word can hold a memory address, and this fact brings us back to HELLO at memory location 012B where we have a memory address that we want to modify.

Modifying *HELLO.COM*

Load HELLO.COM into memory under DDT with the command

      DDT HELLO.COM

In response to this command, CCP will load DDT into memory and start it, and then DDT will load HELLO.COM. Finally, DDT will display a prompt (–) to show that it is waiting for a command. Use the DDT "set", or substitute, command in the form

      S122

followed by carriage return, to examine memory starting at location 0122. In response to this command you should get the display

      0122 0E

At this time, DDT is holding memory location 0122 open for modification. To close location 0122 unmodified and open location 0123, simply press carriage return. You should get the response

      0123 09

Continue to advance through the program code by pressing carriage return until you get to location 012A where you should find

012A C3

This is the op-code of the instruction JMP 0000. We are going to change this instruction so that instead of jumping to 0000, the program will jump to 0100.

Press carriage return to advance to memory location 012B. The display should be

012B 00

This is the low-order byte of the operand. Since we need to change the high-order byte of the operand, press carriage return again. Now the display should be

012C 00

Type 01 (that is, "zero-one") and then press carriage return. DDT will store 01 in location 012C and then advance to location 012D. Enter a blank with the space-bar and then press carriage return. Doing so will end the set command and return DDT to command-mode. DDT should respond with a question mark (?) and then a dash (–). The dash is the command-mode prompt.

Reviewing the Modified Program

Use the DDT list command in the form

L122,12C

to check the modified program. DDT will display assembly language mnemonics representing the machine code starting at location 0122. The display should look like this:

```
0122   MVI C,09
0124   LXI D,0141
0127   CALL 0005
012A   JMP 0100
012D
```

The main thing to verify is that the modified instruction at location 012A is indeed JMP 0100 and not JMP 0001. If we were to execute an instruction to jump to 0001, your program, and CP/M also, would lose control of the computer. A jump to location 0001 would execute the contents of location 0001 as an op-code, no matter what they were intended to be. Location 0001 actually contains the low-order byte of an address. The results that would be created are predictable in principle but chaos in practice, with the near certainty of destruction of information in memory and possibly of information on disk.

The DDT list command

L12A,12C

should display the modified instruction as

012A JMP 0100

whereas the DDT dump command

D12A,12C

will show the address bytes as they are actually stored in memory, with the low-order byte first:

012A C3 00 01

Saving the Modified Program

Get out of DDT with Control-C. When CCP regains control, use the SAVE command in the form

SAVE 2 XHELLO.COM

to create a new command file named XHELLO that contains our modified version of HELLO. This command will save two pages of memory starting at location 0100 and ending at location 02FF.

Now use the command

SAVE 3 YHELLO.COM

to create the file YHELLO.COM containing three pages of memory. This file will be an image of memory starting at location 0100 and extending through memory location 03FF. In other words, this command saves all of memory pages 1, 2, and 3.

Now save four pages of memory in a file named ZHELLO.COM with the command

SAVE 4 ZHELLO.COM

How much space is taken on the disk by each of these files? We can get an answer to this question by calling STAT with the command

STAT ?HELLO.COM

CCP will load and start STAT, and then STAT will create a display such as the following:

Recs	Bytes	Ext	Acc
4	1k	1	R/W A:XHELLO.COM
6	1k	1	R/W A:YHELLO.COM
8	1k	1	R/W A:ZHELLO.COM

The term *Recs* refers to the number of records in the file. The term *record* has many definitions. The text of a person's name and address could be a record. One line of text terminating in a carriage return could be a record. Any user's program running under CP/M can decide for itself the definition and the size of a record. But within the operating system code of CP/M itself, the term *record* has a strict definition. A CP/M record is always 128 bytes. On disk, one memory page of 256 bytes will occupy two CP/M records. Thus, when we save two pages, CP/M writes four CP/M records.

The Bytes column in the STAT display shows how much disk space each file consumes. Although XHELLO.COM occupies only four CP/M records, or 512 bytes, and YHELLO.COM occupies six CP/M records, or 768 bytes, each file consumes 1024 bytes, or 1k of disk space—the same amount consumed by ZHELLO.COM, which occupies eight CP/M records.

Space for eight CP/M records, or 1024 bytes, or 1k is the smallest amount of disk space reservable on any CP/M system. If you are running on a system that has higher capacity disks—that is, disks with storage capacity greater than the storage capacity of the CP/M standard 8-inch single-density floppy disk—then the minimum *storage block* on your system is probably larger than 1k. If this is the case, your STAT display will show that each file consumes 2k, 4k, 8k, or possibly even 16k. The size of the minimum storage block was selected by the system integrator who installed CP/M on your computer.

Information on the storage capacity of a CP/M 2.2 disk and its configuration can be displayed by the STAT command

STAT DSK:

The second line of the display gives the disk's total storage capacity in CP/M records. The next line gives the same information expressed in k units. The last line gives the disk directory size. The CP/M directory size can range from 32 to 8192 directory entries. The line labeled "Records/Block" gives the size, in CP/M records, of the minimum disk storage block. To calculate the block size in bytes, multiply the number of records per block by 128.

To discover how much disk storage space is actually unreserved, or available, at this moment, use an unqualified STAT command. The response should look something like the following:

A: R/W, Space: 84K

In this example, the current disk is drive A, on which CP/M will permit writing, and the available unreserved disk space is 84k, or 86,016 bytes. This space will hold 672 CP/M records.

To increase the amount of disk space available, we can erase any files we don't need. Two files that we currently do not need are YHELLO.COM and ZHELLO.COM. Erase the former with the command

ERA YHELLO.COM

Now use a STAT command to verify that the disk space available has indeed been increased. The available disk space always increases or decreases by a minimum of one block.

Erase the file ZHELLO.COM with the command

ERA ZHELLO.COM

and again check your available disk space.

Testing the Modified Program

Call your modified program with the command

XHELLO

If you've introduced the *patch* correctly, your program will engage you in a conversation of astonishing persistence, if little variety. System control can be returned to CCP with Control-C provided that it is the first character typed in response to the question.

Get out of XHELLO with Control-C, and then call it again with the command

XHELLO

Use Control-E to advance to a new display line without using carriage return. Type the character string

01234567890123456789890123 . . .

continuing for as many characters as XHELLO will accept. Verify that XHELLO will accept 64 characters. Restore the display to a new line with Control-E, and try the same experiment again.

Verify that

0123456789012345678901234567890 1

is the longest string XHELLO will now accept. The buffer size, which is defined by the contents of memory location 0145, evidently has been changed from 65 to 32. The problem, of course, is that we have stored an ASCII blank, 20 hex or 32 decimal, in location 0145 on the first trip through the program. We need to restore the contents of location 0145 to 65, or 41 hex, before looping back to re-execute the program. The straightforward thing to do would be to modify the file HELLO.ASM and reassemble it, but suppose that HELLO is an extremely large program, or suppose that we don't have the source file for HELLO. The patching method we will now introduce is useful in either case.

Patching with the Editor and Assembler

Get out of XHELLO with Control-C, and call the editor with the command

ED PATCH.ASM

The editor should respond NEW FILE and display the command-mode prompt (*). Put the editor into input-mode with i followed by carriage return, and then type the text shown in Fig. 8.1. Then get out of input-mode with Control-Z, and end the edit session with the E command.

```
;File:   PATCH.ASM
;        Patch HELLO to correct buffer size.
;
         ORG     012AH
         JMP     PATCH
;
         ORG     0145H
BUF:     DS      65
PATCH:   MVI     A,65
         STA     BUF
         JMP     100H     ;Loop until control- C
```

Fig. 8.1 Text for HELLO patch

Assemble the patch with the command

ASM PATCH

This will create PATCH.PRN and PATCH.HEX. If there are any assembly errors, carefully compare your PATCH.PRN listing with the listing in Fig. 8.2, correct PATCH.ASM, and reassemble.

When you have an error-free assembly, call DDT with the command

DDT HELLO.COM

The machine code of HELLO is now in memory and can be patched simply by "overlaying" it with the hex file PATCH.HEX. To do so, use the DDT commands

IPATCH.HEX
R

Now use the DDT command

L12A,12C

and verify that the jump instruction at location 012A jumps to location 0186, the location of our patch code. Then use the DDT command

L186,18D

to verify that the patch has indeed been loaded into memory as indicated in assembly listing PATCH.PRN. Get out of DDT with Control-C, and then save the patched program with the command

SAVE 2 XHELLO.COM

```
              ;File:   PATCH.ASM
              ;        Patch HELLO to correct buffer size.
              ;
012A                   ORG     012AH
012A C38601            JMP     PATCH
              ;
0145                   ORG     0145H
0145          BUF:     DS      65
0186 3E41     PATCH:   MVI     A,65
0188 324501            STA     BUF
018B C30001            JMP     100H     ;Loop until control- C
```

Fig. 8.2 Assembly listing of HELLO patch

Call XHELLO with the command

XHELLO

and then use the string 01234567890123 . . . to verify that the patched program will always accept 64 characters.

Summary

Exercises in this chapter have presented two methods for modifying a CP/M command file. Each method is based on loading the file under DDT. Then we can either use the set, or substitute, command to introduce changes from the keyboard or the read command to overlay portions of the program that we wish to modify.

CHAPTER **9**

The Original CP/M Disk

CP/M WAS ORIGINALLY designed for the 8-inch single-density IBM 3740 format floppy disk. Discussion of CP/M's handling of this single-density disk remains necessary for two reasons. First, the 8-inch single-density disk is a standard medium for the distribution of CP/M software. Second, all higher capacity CP/M disk processing operations are based on extensions of the prototype structure set down for processing the single-density disk.

The IBM Single-Density Disk

The IBM 3740 disk has 77 tracks numbered 0 through 76 in decimal, or 00 through 4C in hex. Each track contains 26 sectors numbered 1 through 26 in decimal, or 01 through 1A in hex. Each sector contains 128 or 80 hex eight-bit bytes.

Disk Format

The IBM 3740 format is called *soft sectored*. This means that the disk has to be formatted before it can be used. To *format* a disk means to write 26 IBM-prescribed sector preambles and postambles on each track of the disk, leaving space—by writing *filler bytes*—between each preamble and postamble for 128 bytes of data, with enough room to allow those 128 bytes to be written in later without destroying a preamble. Each sector preamble contains that sector's track number and sector number. The postamble primarily provides the space needed to allow write-head current turn-off before encountering the next preamble. The filler byte used in the data space is hex E5.

Most disk controllers provide a disk formatting facility. This facility is ordinarily made available to the user through a utility program supplied by the computer manufacturer or system integrator.

The formatting operation physically erases all previous information, if any, that may have been written on the disk. A *blank disk* is unformatted. An *empty disk* is formatted but contains no other information.

The CP/M Partition

CP/M partitions the disk into two areas—a *system area* and a *user area*. The system area of the standard single-density disk consists of tracks 00 and 01. The user area consists of tracks 02 through 76.

The Reserve Block

The user space is divided into *reserve blocks*. A reserve block is the smallest portion of disk space that can be reserved, or allocated. The size of the reserve block on the standard CP/M single-density disk is eight CP/M sectors, or 1024 bytes. Since we have 1950 CP/M sectors in the user space (75 tracks of 26 sectors each), we have 243.75 reserve blocks (1950/8) in the user space. These 243 blocks are numbered 00 through F2 in hex. The fractional block of six sectors is not used.

A standard single-density disk has blocks 00 and 01 reserved for the disk directory. An empty disk thus provides 241 blocks, or 241k bytes, of storage space. Block 02, the first user-file block, is on track 02. Block 03 is partly on track 02 and partly on track 03. Block boundaries generally do not coincide with track boundaries.

Disk Directory

Each directory entry occupies 32 bytes. One CP/M sector can hold four such 32-byte entries. Since there are two blocks of eight sectors each reserved for the directory, the CP/M standard single-density disk has room for exactly 64 directory entries.

It is easy to change directory size. Under CP/M 2.2, the directory size is defined by entries in a table residing in CBIOS. Under CP/M 1.4, all you have to do is change a few bytes in BDOS. The complications are operational. Under CP/M 1.4, for example, once you've changed your BDOS to increase the size of the directory, you must treat as Read-Only any disk written by a standard BDOS. Details for modifying CP/M 1.4 directory size are included in Appendix D.

Summary

Even though most CP/M systems now use higher capacity disks, an understanding of the original 8-inch single-density format remains valuable because the original format continues to be used for distribution of CP/M software, and CP/M's handling of higher capacity formats can be explained in terms of the original structure.

CHAPTER 10

Swapping Disks

A SYSTEM DISK is a formatted disk with a copy of the CP/M resident written on the system tracks. On most CP/M systems, the utility program called SYSGEN can be used to create duplicates of your system disk. Detailed directions for using SYSGEN can be found in the Digital Research manual, "An Introduction to CP/M Features and Facilities" (page 27).

Since reading and writing the system portion of a disk is actually a hardware dependent operation, your system integrator may have provided a program other than SYSGEN for this purpose. If a program other than SYSGEN is used, detailed directions for creating system disks will be found in the documentation provided by your computer manufacturer or system integrator.

For the exercise in this chapter, you will need one disk drive and two system disks. To learn how to mount and dismount the disk in the disk drive, either ask someone to show you how or review the directions provided by the manufacturer or system integrator.

In this exercise, we will write a program and then put a copy of the command file for this program on each of the two disks. Then we will use this program to demonstrate what happens—or, more accurately, what doesn't happen—when you swap disks.

The program called RBRDIS shown in Fig. 10.1 displays CP/M's disk allocation table, a table created in memory by CP/M and used to keep track of those blocks of the disk that are occupied by files and those that are "free," or available. We will usually refer to this table as the *Record Block Reservation*, or *RBR, table*.

```
                    ;File:   RBRDIS.ASM
                    ;
                    ;       Display disk allocation table.
                    ;
                    ;       CP/M call:
                    ;
                    ;                       RBRDIS d:
                    ;
0100                        ORG 100H
0100 210000                 LXI H,0
0103 39                     DAD SP
0104 22BB01                 SHLD OLDSP
0107 315101                 LXI SP,STACK
010A C3BE01                 JMP DRB
                    ;
                    ;       Data space.
                    ;
010D 0000           BLMAX:  DW      0       ;Maximum Block number
010F 0000           RBRFWA: DW      0       ;Allocation table fwa
                    ;
0111                        DS      2*32
0151 =              STACK   EQU     $
                    ;
                    ;       Assembly constants.
                    ;
0005 =              BDOS    EQU     0005    ;CP/M entry point
005C =              FCB     EQU     005CH   ;CP/M default file control block
                    ;
                    ;       Subroutines.
                    ;
                    ;       EOL - End of Line.
                    ;       Issue CR, LF
                    ;
0151 E5D5C5         EOL:    PUSH H ! PUSH D ! PUSH B
0154 1E0A                   MVI E,0AH
0156 CD6201                 CALL DCH
0159 1E0D                   MVI E,0DH
015B CD6201                 CALL DCH
015E C1D1E1                 POP B ! POP D ! POP H
0161 C9                     RET
                    ;
                    ;       DCH - Display Character.
                    ;       Entry   E = character
                    ;
0162 0E02           DCH:    MVI C,2
0164 CD0500                 CALL BDOS
0167 C9                     RET
                    ;
                    ;       SDD - Select Disk Drive.
                    ;
0168 3A5C00         SDD:    LDA FCB
016B B7                     ORA A
016C C8                     RZ              ;If no selection
                    ;
016D 3D                     DCR A
016E 5F                     MOV E,A
016F 0E0E                   MVI C,14
0171 CD0500                 CALL BDOS
0174 C9                     RET
                    ;
                    ;       GRA - Get RBR address.
                    ;       Exit    HL = Allocation table fwa
                    ;
0175 0E1B           GRA:    MVI C,27
0177 CD0500                 CALL BDOS
017A C9                     RET
                    ;
                    ;       GMB - Get Maximum Block number.
                    ;       Exit    HL = max block number
                    ;
017B 0E0C           GMB:    MVI C,12        ;Check CP/M version
017D CD0500                 CALL BDOS
0180 7D                     MOV A,L
0181 B7                     ORA A
0182 21F300                 LXI H,243
0185 C8                     RZ              ;If CP/M 1.4
```

Fig. 10.1 *Assembly listing of RBDRIS*

```
                       ;
0186  0E1F                         MVI   C,31
0188  CD0500                       CALL  BDOS
018B  110500                       LXI   D,5
018E  19                           DAD   D
018F  5E                           MOV   E,M
0190  23                           INX   H
0191  56                           MOV   D,M
0192  EB                           XCHG
0193  23                           INX   H
0194  C9                           RET
                       ;
                       ;           D8B - Display Eight Bits.
                       ;           Entry   A = byte to be displayed
0195  E5D5       D8B:              PUSH  H ! PUSH D
0197  1608                         MVI   D,8
0199  B7         D8B1:             ORA   A
019A  D5                           PUSH  D
019B  F5                           PUSH  PSW
019C  CDA901                       CALL  D1B          ;Display one bit
019F  F1                           POP   PSW
01A0  17                           RAL
01A1  D1                           POP   D
01A2  15                           DCR   D
01A3  C29901                       JNZ   D8B1         ;Loop for 8 bits
                       ;
01A6  D1E1                         POP   D ! POP H
01A8  C9                           RET
                       ;
                       ;           D1B - Display One Bit.
                       ;           Entry   A, high bit = bit to display
                       ;
01A9  B7         D1B:              ORA   A
01AA  1E31                         MVI   E,'1'
01AC  C5                           PUSH  B
01AD  FAB201                       JM    D1B1         ;If bit set
01B0  1E30                         MVI   E,'0'
01B2  CD6201     D1B1:             CALL  DCH
01B5  C1                           POP   B
01B6  0B                           DCX   B            ;Advance block count
01B7  79                           MOV   A,C
01B8  B0                           ORA   B
01B9  C0                           RNZ                ;If not end of RBR
                       ;
01BA  310000                       LXI   SP,0
01BB  =          OLDSP             EQU   $-2
01BD  C9                           RET
                       ;
                       ;           Main Program.
                       ;
01BE  CDE501     DRB:              CALL  HDG          ;Make a heading
01C1  CD6801                       CALL  SDD          ;Select disk
01C4  CD7501                       CALL  GRA          ;Set HL=RBR fwa
01C7  220F01                       SHLD  RBRFWA
01CA  E5                           PUSH  H
01CB  CD7B01                       CALL  GMB          ;Set HL=max block
01CE  220D01                       SHLD  BLMAX
01D1  4D                           MOV   C,L
01D2  44                           MOV   B,H
01D3  E1                           POP   H
                       ;
01D4  1608       DRB1:             MVI   D,8
01D6  7E         DRB2:             MOV   A,M          ;Display RBR bits
01D7  CD9501                       CALL  D8B
01DA  23                           INX   H
01DB  15                           DCR   D
01DC  C2D601                       JNZ   DRB2         ;If not end of one line
01DF  CD5101                       CALL  EOL
01E2  C3D401                       JMP   DRB1         ;Loop to end of RBR
                       ;
                       ;           HDG - Display a heading.
                       ;
01E5  3A5C00     HDG:              LDA   FCB
01E8  B7                           ORA   A
01E9  C2EE01                       JNZ   HDG1         ;If  d:  used
01EC  3E01                         MVI   A,1
```

Fig. 10.1 *Assembly listing of RBDRIS (Cont.)*

```
01EE  C640      HDG1:   ADI  40H
01F0  320B02            STA  HDGB
01F3  11FC01            LXI  D,HDGA
01F6  0E09              MVI  C,9
01F8  CD0500            CALL BDOS
01FB  C9                RET
                 ;
01FC  2020202020HDGA:   DB      '          Disk '
020B  413A205265HDGB:   DB      'A: Record Block Reservation (RBR) Table.'
0233  0D0A24            DB      0DH,0AH,'$'
```

Fig. 10.1 *Assembly listing of RBDRIS (Cont.)*

Displaying the RBR

Using the name RBRDIS or a name of your own choosing, call the editor with the command

ED RBRDIS.ASM

to create the assembly language text file for RBRDIS. Having created many such text files in previous exercises, you should have no trouble creating RBRDIS.ASM from the assembly listing in Fig. 10.1.

Assemble your program with the command

ASM RBRDIS

If there are assembly errors, carefully compare your assembly listing with that in Fig. 10.1. Edit and reassemble until you have an error-free assembly. Then create the command file RBRDIS.COM with the command

LOAD RBRDIS

When you call this program with the command

RBRDIS

it should create a display of ones and zeros such as that shown in Fig. 10.2. This table contains a bit for each CP/M record block on the disk, and its size will therefore depend on the size of the disk. The 243-bit table of Fig. 10.2 corresponds to the 243 record blocks on a CP/M standard 8-inch single-density disk.

The Record Block Table (RBT)

The RBR table in memory is created by CP/M from the record block names that appear in the file directory on the disk and resides in the main memory of your computer, not on the disk. As new files are written, bits are set in the

```
            Disk A: Record Block Reservation (RBR) Table.
    1111111111111111111111111111111111111111111111111111111111111111
    111111111111111111111100000000000000000000000000000000000000000
    0000000000000000000000000000000000000000000000000000000000000000
    0000000000000000000000000000000000000000000000000
```

Fig. 10.2 *Example of RBR display for a CP/M standard single-density disk*

RBR—to reserve used blocks—and when the file is closed, the names of the blocks are copied from the file control block in memory to the *Record Block Table (RBT)* in the directory on the disk.

Testing the Effect of Swapping

If you have a printer on your system, you may wish to put CP/M into console-print mode with Control-P in order to create hard-copy listings of the RBR displays created in this exercise.

Examine the current RBR with the command

> *RBRDIS*

Then create a new file with the command

> *SAVE 1 TEMP.XXX*

and again examine the RBR with the command

> *RBRDIS*

You should find that one of the bits in the RBR has changed from zero to one. This bit reserves the block now occupied by TEMP.XXX.

Each bit in the table has a name. The name of the first bit is 00; the name of the second is 01; the name of the third is 02; and so on. Note that the name of the bit in the RBR is the same as the name of the record block that it reserves.

Now erase the file with the command

> *ERA TEMP.XXX*

and examine the RBR with the command

> *RBRDIS*

The RBR bit that was set for TEMP.XXX should now be clear, i.e. reset to zero.

Dismount the disk that you have been using—we will call it Disk-1—and replace it with your other system disk, Disk-2. Since the CP/M residents on these two disks should be identical, we can *warmboot* (see "An Explanation of Terms" in Chap. 12) the new disk with Control-C. This operation does not modify the transient program area, where we still have an image of RBRDIS in memory. Now use the command

> *SAVE 3 RBRDIS.COM*

to create on Disk-2 an executable command file for RBRDIS.

Examine the RBR table of Disk-2 with the command

> *RBRDIS*

We are now prepared to exhibit a property of CP/M that has in the past been responsible for a good deal of confusion. Since Disk-2 is mounted at this time, we have before us a display of its RBR table. Examine it carefully.

Now remove Disk-2 and remount Disk-1. Without doing anything else, type

RBRDIS

and press carriage return. The RBR table displayed by this command is the RBR currently in memory. If we were to write on the disk at this moment, it is this table that would be used to determine the location of a free block on the disk. If you examine this RBR carefully, you will discover that even though Disk-1 is now mounted, the RBR table in memory is the table that corresponds to Disk-2.

Warmboot the system with Control-C, and then redisplay the RBR with the command

RBRDIS

The RBR displayed this time should be the table that corresponds to the disk that is actually installed, Disk-1.

Now dismount Disk-1 and reinstall Disk-2. Without doing anything else, attempt to create a file on Disk-2 with the command

SAVE 3 TEMP.XXX

CP/M will probably respond with the message

BDOS ERR ON A:R/O

What this message means is that CP/M has detected that the RBR in memory does not correspond to that of the disk actually mounted. When CP/M detects this situation, it declares the disk to be Read-Only.

Use Control-C to warmboot the system, thus causing CP/M to rebuild the RBR from the directory of the disk actually present.

Disk Log-In

CP/M maintains an RBR table in memory for each disk drive that the system has available. When the system is first started with a coldboot, or restarted with a warmboot, CP/M clears all RBR tables and then logs in the disk in the current drive, usually drive A. To *log in* a disk means to build the RBR in memory from the record block names that appear in the RBT of the directory on the disk.

Immediately after log-in, the RBR in memory corresponds exactly, or is perfectly synchronized with, the RBT on the disk. In other words, for each record block name that appears in the RBT on the disk, there is a bit set to one in the RBR in memory. This synchronism disappears when a file is written.

Summary

When a file is opened, the RBT entry for the file—that is, the second half of the directory entry for the file—is copied into a file control block in memory. When information is written into the file, causing additional blocks to be reserved, bits are set in the RBR in memory to reserve the blocks. As blocks are reserved, their names are entered into the RBT image in the file control block in memory; the names are not entered into the RBT on the disk. The actual RBT on the disk is updated only when the file is closed.

Under CP/M, the primary purpose for the operation called *close* is to copy the RBT image from the file control block in memory to the RBT on the disk. CP/M files are not "chained," or otherwise "threaded." No sector, block, or extent contains the starting address of the next one. Disk address information exists on the CP/M disk only in the CP/M directory. Unless the RBT in the directory on the disk contains the name of every block occupied by the file, no way exists to piece the file together. In other words, a readable file exists on the CP/M disk when, and only when, it has been successfully closed.

11

Disk Files

CP/M PARTITIONS EVERY disk into two areas—one reserved for an image of the CP/M resident and the other for the user. A CP/M resident program called BDOS (Basic Disk Operating System) manages the portion of the disk reserved for the user.

File Control Block

The fundamental data structure used to coordinate disk operations between the user and BDOS is the *file control block*. The file control block is essentially an image of the file's directory entry. Its format is illustrated in Fig. 11.1.

Disk Directory

The disk directory is the interlaced merger of two tables. The first half of each entry is an entry in the *File Name Table (FNT)*. The second half of each directory entry is an entry in the *Record Block Table (RBT)*. While you are writing a file, it is the image of the directory entry residing in your file control block that receives all the attention. As you write the file, BDOS reserves disk space for the information written and enters the corresponding reservation block names into the RBT image in your file control block. The directory entry on the disk itself is not updated while you are writing the file. It is updated only when you close the file.

```
File Control Block (FCB) format.

                   0  1  2  3  4  5  6  7  8  9  A  B  C  D  E  F
FNT      0         dr f1 f2 f3 f4 f5 f6 f7 f8 t1 t2 t3 ex 00 s2 rc

RBT      1         d0 d1 d2 d3 d4 d5 d6 d7 d8 d9 da db dc dd de df

         2         nr r1 r2 ov


        dr         disk drive code 00 = no selection, use "current" drive
                                   01 = Drive A
                                   02 = Drive B, etc

        f1-f8      file name

        t1-t3      file type

        ex         low five bits of the logical extent

        s2         low four bits hold the high five bits
                   of the logical extent.
                   high bit of s2 set indicates file not written

        rc         Record Count of the current logical extent,
                   takes on values 0 - 128 (00 to 80 hex)

        d0-df      16 Record Block Reservation bytes, or eight
                   Record Block Reservation words

        nr         Next Record to be accessed in the current extent

        r1,r2      random record number

        ov         overflow return from r1, r2
```

Fig. 11.1 *CP/M 2.2 file control block format*

Disk Access

All CP/M disk operations are actually random access operations. BDOS makes disk operations appear to be sequential by advancing Next Record after each CP/M sector read or write operation. When you perform disk operations using the sequential BDOS functions, BDOS also takes care of opening and closing additional extents as required. On a small-capacity disk, such as the standard 8-inch single-density disk, an extent is the amount of space addressed by one directory entry. Large files are accommodated by using additional directory entries. Each additional directory entry, of course, is half FNT and half RBT. The FNT half is a copy of FNT(0)—that is, the FNT of the "zeroth" extent— whereas the RBT half stores names of the additional reservation blocks occupied by the file. All extents of a given file are numbered for order identification by the value in byte 0C of the FNT entry, called the *extent byte*.

Sequential Access

If you issue a write command to BDOS, with Next Record in the file control block set to 7F, BDOS will write the CP/M sector, then close the current extent, open the next extent, and set Next Record in your file control block to 00.

If you issue a read command to BDOS with Next Record in the file control block set to 80 hex, BDOS will open the next extent, set Next Record to 00, read the first record of the new extent, and then advance Next Record in your file control block to 01.

Next Record of a read request must point to a CP/M sector that is within the file. Next Record of a write request can point anywhere. Whenever Next Record of a write request points to an empty space in the RBT image in your file control block, BDOS simply reserves an available record block, writes your CP/M sector in that block, and fills in the RBT space in your file control block accordingly.

Random Access

It is important to understand that the only thing BDOS really knows about your file is what it learns by reading information from your file control block. By properly setting up a file control block, you can read any sector you wish to read, or write any sector you wish to write, and in any order. For example, to read the one-thousandth CP/M sector, or record, of a file, it isn't necessary to read sequentially through 999 records first. All we have to do is calculate which extent holds the one-thousandth record, open that extent, set Next Record in the file control block to point directly to the record of interest, and then issue a sequential record read request to BDOS.

Since the first record of a file is record number zero (0), the one-thousandth record of the file is record number 999. Record number 999 decimal is 3E7 hex or 0011 1110 0111 binary. The low-order seven bits are 110 0111, or 67 hex. The high-order five bits are 0 0111, or 07 hex. To read record number 999, all we have to do is open extent 07 hex, set Next Record to 67 hex, and read.

Writing is just as easy. The only difference is that if the extent doesn't exist, then we "create" it rather than "open" it.

Random Access Exercise

The program named RANDOMEX (RANDOM disk access Exercise) shown in Fig. 11.2 provides a working example of this CP/M 1.4 style of random disk access. This program will run under either CP/M 1.4 or CP/M 2.2.

The BDOS of CP/M 2.2 provides special random access read and write functions that automatically calculate Next Record, and the needed extent, from a 16-bit record number provided in bytes 11 and 12 (hex) of the file control block. Compatibility between the two styles of random access operation is limited to extents 00 through 1F hex because CP/M 2.2 stores only the low-order five bits of the extent number in byte 0C of the directory entry. Under CP/M 1.4, the extent byte can take on values from 00 through FF hex. Any new application program needing random access should take advantage of the new CP/M 2.2 random access functions. We will use the old style random access method in this exercise because the old style visibly exhibits the fundamentals of the process and it works under both CP/M versions, 1.4 and 2.2.

```
                    ;File:   RAMDOMEX.ASM
                    ;
                    ;        Random access disk exercise.
                    ;
  0100              ORG 100H
  0100 314902       LXI SP,STACK
  0103 118801       LXI D,DMA        ;Set record buffer address
  0106 0E1A         MVI C,26
  0108 CD0500       CALL bdos
  010B C34902       JMP RAD
                    ;
                    ;        Data space.
                    ;
  010E 00      FCB: DB      0
  010F 5445535446   DB      'TESTFILETMP',0,0,0,0
  011E 0000000000   DB      0,0,0,0,0,0,0,0,0,0,0,0,0,0,0,0
  012E 00000000     DB      0,0,0,0
  0132 00     NXTR: DB      0        ;temp for next record
  0050 =           cbufs equ  80     ;console buffer size
  0133 50    CBUFF: DB      cbufs    ;console buffer
  0134              DS      cbufs+2
  0186 00           DB      0        ;Buffer size
  0187 00           DB      0        ;Character count
  0188       DMA:   DS      128
  0208 24           DB      '$'
  0209              DS      32*2     ;space for 32 "pushes"
  0249     STACK:   DS      0
                    ;
                    ;        ASSEMBLY CONSTANTS.
                    ;
  000D =     CR     EQU     0DH
  000A =     LF     EQU     0AH
  011A =     EXT    EQU     FCB+0CH ;EXTENT
  011C =     S2     EQU     FCB+0EH ;"s2"
  012E =     NR     EQU     FCB+20H ;NEXT RECORD
  0005 =     bdos   equ     0005     ;BDOS vector
                    ;
                    ;        RAD - Random Access Disk exercise.
                    ;
  0249 118302 RAD:  LXI D,RADA       ;"Record number:"
  024C CD1B04       CALL MSG
  024F CDA303       CALL RCB         ;Read console response
  0252 CDF803       CALL ADV         ;Assemble decimal value
  0255 CDE803       CALL PRN         ;Process record number
                    ;
  0258 321C01       STA S2           ;Set "s2" for 2.2
  025B 211A01       LXI H,ext        ;Set file extent
  025E 70           MOV M,B
  025F 213201       LXI H,NXTR       ;Save "next record"
  0262 71           MOV M,C
                    ;
  0263 119502       LXI D,RADB       ;"Read or Write?"
  0266 CD1B04       CALL MSG
  0269 CDA303       CALL RCB         ;Read console response
  026C 3A3501       LDA CBUFF+2
  026F CD1504       CALL UCC
  0272 FE57         CPI 'W'
  0274 CA7D02       JZ RAD1          ;If write
                    ;
                    ;        Process random read.
                    ;
  0277 CDAD02       CALL PRR         ;Read random record
  027A C34902       JMP RAD
                    ;
                    ;        Process random write.
                    ;
  027D CDE102 RAD1: CALL PRW         ;Write random record
  0280 C34902       JMP RAD
                    ;
  0283 0D0A526563RADA: DB    cr,lf,'Record number: $'
  0295 0A52656164RADB: DB    lf,'Read or Write? (R/W): $'
                    ;
                    ;        PRR - Process Random Read.
                    ;
  02AD CDBD03 PRR:  CALL OPN         ;Open file
  02B0 CAC902       JZ PRR2          ;If no file
```

Fig. 11.2 *Assembly listing of RANDOMEX*

```
02B3 3A3201                 LDA   NXTR         ;Set "next record"
02B6 322E01                 STA   nr
02B9 CDC803                 CALL  RDC          ;Read record
02BC C2C902                 JNZ   PRR2         ;If read error
              ;
02BF 118701                 LXI   D,DMA-1      ;Display record text
02C2 3E0A                   MVI   A,lf
02C4 12                     STAX  D
02C5 CD1B04    PRR1:        CALL  MSG
02C8 C9                     RET
              ;
              ;             Process no-file-found, or read-error.
              ;
02C9 11CF02    PRR2:        LXI   D,PRRA       ;"Record empty."
02CC C3C502                 JMP   PRR1
              ;
02CF 0A5265636FPRRA:        DB       1f,'Record is empty.$'
              ;
              ;             PRW - Process Random Write.
              ;
02E1 CDD203    PRW:         CALL  SFF          ;Search for file
02E4 C2F002                 JNZ   PRW1         ;If found
              ;
02E7 CDDD03                 CALL  MKF          ;Create file
02EA CA1103                 JZ    PRW3         ;If no directory space
              ;
02ED C3F302                 JMP   PRW2
02F0 CDBD03    PRW1:        CALL  OPN          ;Open existing file
02F3 3A3201    PRW2:        LDA   NXTR         ;Set "next record"
02F6 322E01                 STA   nr
02F9 CD7303                 CALL  RRT          ;Read record text from console
              ;
              ;             Write the record.
              ;
02FC 110E01                 LXI   D,FCB
02FF 0E15                   MVI   C,21
0301 CD0500                 CALL  bdos
0304 B7                     ORA   A
0305 C21103                 JNZ   PRW3         ;If write error
              ;
0308 110E01                 LXI   D,FCB        ;Close file
030B 0E10                   MVI   C,16
030D CD0500                 CALL  bdos
0310 C9                     RET
              ;
0311 114303    PRW3:        LXI   D,PRWB       ;"Write error"
0314 CD1B04    PRW4:        CALL  MSG
0317 C9                     RET
              ;
0318 115503    PRW5:        LXI   D,PRWC       ;"No directory space."
031B C31403                 JMP   PRW4
              ;
031E 0D0A456E74PRWA:        DB       cr,lf,'Enter your text for this record:',cr,lf,'$'
0343 4469736B20PRWB:        DB       'Disk write error.$'
0355 4E6F206469PRWC:        DB       'No directory space available.$'
              ;
              ;             RRT - Read record text from console.
              ;
0373 CD9603    RRT:         CALL  BFB          ;Blank fill buffer
0376 111E03                 LXI   D,PRWA       ;"Record text:"
0379 CD1B04                 CALL  MSG
037C 3E7F                   MVI   A,127
037E 328601                 STA   dma-2
0381 118601                 LXI   D,dma-2
0384 0E0A                   MVI   C,10
0386 CD0500                 CALL  bdos
0389 3A8701                 LDA   dma-1        ;Put "$" at text end
038C 5F                     MOV   E,A
038D 1600                   MVI   D,0
038F 218801                 LXI   H,dma
0392 19                     DAD   D
0393 3624                   MVI   M,'$'
0395 C9                     RET
              ;
              ;             BFB - Blank Fill Buffer.
```

Fig. 11.2 *Assembly listing of RANDOMEX (Cont.)*

```
                          ;
0396  218801  BFB:        LXI  H,DMA        ;Buffer fwa
0399  0E80                MVI  C,128
039B  3620    BFB1:       MVI  M,' '
039D  23                  INX  H
039E  0D                  DCR  C
039F  C29B03              JNZ  BFB1         ;Loop for 128 bytes
03A2  C9                  RET
                          ;
                          ;        RCB - Read Console Buffer.
                          ;        Exit   CBUFF loaded with text line from console
                          ;
03A3  3E50    RCB:        MVI  A,cbufs      ;Reset buffer
03A5  113301              LXI  D,CBUFF
03A8  12                  STAX D
03A9  0E0A                MVI  C,10         ;Read console line
03AB  CD0500              CALL bdos
03AE  213401              LXI  H,CBUFF+1
03B1  5E                  MOV  E,M          ;Char count
03B2  23                  INX  H
03B3  7E                  MOV  A,M          ;1st char
03B4  1600                MVI  D,0
03B6  19                  DAD  D
03B7  3624                MVI  M,'$'
03B9  213501              LXI  H,CBUFF+2
03BC  C9                  RET
                          ;
                          ;        OPN - Open File.
                          ;        Exit   Z = true, if file not found
                          ;
03BD  110E01  OPN:        LXI  D,fcb
03C0  0E0F                MVI  C,15
03C2  CD0500              CALL bdos
03C5  FEFF                CPI  0FFH
03C7  C9                  RET
                          ;
                          ;        RDC - Read Record.
                          ;        Exit   Z = true, if no errors
                          ;
03C8  110E01  RDC:        LXI  D,FCB
03CB  0E14                MVI  C,20
03CD  CD0500              CALL bdos
03D0  B7                  ORA  A
03D1  C9                  RET
                          ;
                          ;        SFF = Search for File.
                          ;        Exit   Z = true, if file not found
                          ;
03D2  110E01  SFF:        LXI  D,fcb
03D5  0E11                MVI  C,17
03D7  CD0500              CALL bdos
03DA  FEFF                CPI  0FFH
03DC  C9                  RET
                          ;
                          ;        MKF - Make new File.
                          ;        Exit   Z = true, if no directory space
                          ;
03DD  110E01  MKF:        LXI  D,fcb
03E0  0E16                MVI  C,22
03E2  CD0500              CALL bdos
03E5  FEFF                CPI  0FFH
03E7  C9                  RET
                          ;
                          ;        PRN - Process Record Number.
                          ;        Entry  HL = logical record number
                          ;        Exit   C = "next record"
                          ;               B = current "extent"
                          ;
03E8  3E7F    PRN:        MVI  A,7FH
03EA  A5                  ANA  L
03EB  4F                  MOV  C,A          ;next record
03EC  3EF0                MVI  A,0F0H       ;Get "s2"
03EE  A4                  ANA  H
03EF  5F                  MOV  E,A
03F0  29                  DAD  H            ;shift HL one bit left
03F1  44                  MOV  B,H
03F2  7B                  MOV  A,E
```

Fig. 11.2 *Assembly listing of RANDOMEX (Cont.)*

```
03F3 1F1F1F1F              RAR ! RAR ! RAR ! RAR
03F7 C9                    RET
                      ;
                      ;
                      ;
                      ;        ADV - Assemble Decimal Value.
                      ;        Entry   HL = ASCII string fwa
                      ;        Exit    HL = hex value
                      ;                DE = next string location
                      ;                 B = terminating non-hex char
                      ;                 C = hex digit count
                      ;
03F8 EB               ADV:   XCHG
03F9 210000                  LXI H,0000          ;Clear assembly
03FC 4C                      MOV C,H
                      ;
03FD 1A               ADV1:  LDAX D
03FE 13                      INX D
03FF B7                      ORA A
0400 C8                      RZ                  ;If end of string
                      ;
0401 D630                    SUI '0'
0403 FE0A                    CPI 10
0405 D0                      RNC                 ;If non-numeric
                      ;
0406 29                      DAD H               ;HL=10*HL
0407 4D                      MOV C,L
0408 44                      MOV B,H
0409 29                      DAD H
040A 29                      DAD H
040B 09                      DAD B
040C 85                      ADD L               ;Add new digit
040D 6F                      MOV L,A
040E D2FD03                  JNC ADV1            ;If no carry
0411 24                      INR H
0412 C3FD03                  JMP ADV1
                      ;
                      ;        UCC - Create Upper-case Character.
                      ;
0415 FE60             UCC:   CPI 60H
0417 D8                      RC                  ;If upper-case
0418 D620                    SUI 20H
041A C9                      RET
                      ;
                      ;        MSG - Issue Message to Console.
                      ;        Entry   DE = message address
                      ;
041B 0E09             MSG:   MVI C,9
041D CD0500                  CALL 5
0420 C9                      RET
```

Fig. 11.2 *Assembly listing of RANDOMEX (Cont.)*

Use the editor to create RANDOMEX.ASM by copying the source text from the assembly listing in Fig. 11.2. Assemble your program with the command

ASM RANDOMEX

and then create the command file RANDOMEX.COM by calling the loader with the command

LOAD RANDOMEX

Operation of RANDOMEX

RANDOMEX reads and writes a *scratch file* named TESTFILE.TMP. The program will either create this file or access an existing one. If a file by this name exists and you want to preserve it, either change its name or change the name used by RANDOMEX at FCB:.

When you call this exercise program with the command

RANDOMEX

it will ask first for a record number. Enter a decimal number in the range 0 through 4095. The program will then ask whether you want to read or write this record. Enter W (Write). Any other response will be interpreted as a read request. All records are assumed to contain ASCII-encoded text. The only reason for this restriction is that the record contents are displayed verbatim on the screen.

When a write is requested, the program will read text from the console. Up to 127 characters may be stored in each record. One character space is reserved in the 128-byte CP/M record for a terminating dollar sign ($) to provide for easy display of the record on the screen.

Exercise 1

Erase TESTFILE.TMP and then call RANDOMEX. At its response, "Record number:," type 4095 and press carriage return. Request a record write with W and then type in text—"Record #4095," for example—and then press carriage return. Get out of RANDOMEX with Control-C. Call STAT with the command

STAT TESTFILE.TMP

Most of the information in the response from STAT will be inaccurate, except for the bytes reserved, which should be one record block. STAT does not accurately interpret directory entries created for files written by random access methods. STAT is designed to interpret directory entries created for files written sequentially.

Exercise 2

Restart the test program with the command

RANDOMEX

and then read record number 4095. Write record number zero, using text such as "This is record zero." Then read record number zero and verify its content.

Exercise 3

Write record number 4096, using text such as "Record #4096." Then read record number 4096 and verify its content.

Exercise 4

Read record number zero. If you are running under CP/M 2.2, you will find that record number zero has been overwritten by record number 4096, the reason being that the largest extent number that CP/M 2.2 BDOS will permit is 1F hex, corresponding to logical record number FFF hex, or 4095 decimal. CP/M 2.2 uses a logical extent that is actually a nine-bit value, but it stores only the low five bits of this value in the *ext byte*, or byte 0C, of the directory entry. The high-order four bits are stored in byte s2 or 0E of the directory entry, but BDOS won't use values stored there by the calling program. In order to write record number 4096 and beyond under CP/M 2.2, you must use the CP/M 2.2 BDOS special random access functions.

If you are running under CP/M 1.4, you will find that record number 4096 does not overwrite record number zero. Under CP/M version 1.4, RANDOMEX will read and write distinct records numbered 0 through 32,767 in decimal. The BDOS of CP/M 1.4 permits the extent byte in the directory entry to take on values 00 through FF hex. Compatibility with CP/M 2.2 ends at record number 4095.

Question 1

There is storage space on a standard 8-inch single-density disk for exactly 1928 CP/M records (counting in decimal). How, then, are we able to write a record numbered 4095?

Answer

Decimal number 4095 is FFF in hex and 1111 1111 1111 in binary. The low seven bits give the value 7F hex for Next Record. The high five bits give the value 1F hex for the extent. We simply set these values in our file control block and write. The disk space needed is one directory entry and one record block.

Question 2

Can a file created sequentially be read randomly?

Hint

Try creating a file sequentially by a command such as

PIP TESTFILE.TMP=RANDOMEX.PRN

and then try reading it with RANDOMEX. All CP/M files are readable by random access methods.

Question 3

How could RANDOMEX be modified to read non-ASCII files?

Hint

Delete the record display or change it to a hex display such as that created by the D command of DDT or by the DUMP program described in the Digital Research manual, "CP/M 2.2 Interface Guide" (page 34).

Exercise 5

The DUMP program on page 34 and also the file copy program on page 30 of this Digital Research manual provide examples of CP/M sequential file operations. An example of CP/M 2.2 style random access is also described there (starting at page 38). Create these programs from the listings provided in the manual and test them on your system.

Summary

The program developed in this chapter demonstrates that all CP/M disk operations are random access operations, and by means of the exercise we've explored fully the question of random access compatibility between CP/M 1.4 and CP/M 2.2.

CHAPTER 12

Booting Up

O*NE OF THE* most instructive exercises that can be undertaken to understand any computer system is to examine carefully the detailed procedure by which the system is started up from scratch.

In this chapter we will take a detailed look at the specific start-up process defined and implemented by the Tarbell single-density floppy-disk controller. A specific example is more instructive than a theoretical discussion, especially since all start-up processors must produce the same end result. The CP/M resident must be loaded to preselected locations of upper memory in all CP/M systems no matter what hardware is involved.

Loading the CP/M Resident

The CP/M resident is designed to fit into the space available on two tracks of the CP/M single-density disk. The space available is 6,528 bytes [$(2 \times 26 \times 128) -$ 128]. One sector of 128 bytes—the first sector of the first track—has been reserved for special coldboot use by the disk controller. The task of the disk controller system–start processor is to move the contents of these two system tracks from disk into the top of available memory.

A *bootstrap* technique is used. Disk controller hardware reads the first sector of the first track into memory, and then the program contained in that sector is given control and reads in the remainder of the two system tracks. In any case, no matter what hardware is involved, the end result must be CCP, BDOS, and CBIOS in memory, with linkage to CBIOS placed at location 0000 and linkage to BDOS placed at location 0005.

An Explanation of Terms

Booting up is the name of the process used to load the CP/M resident into your computer's memory. In any discussion of CP/M, the terms *warmboot* and *coldboot* make frequent appearances. A warmboot, or *warmstart*, is what you get when you jump to 0000. A coldboot, or *coldstart*, is what you get when you hit the Reset button. In other words, coldboot, or coldstart, is a process implemented in the hardware and warmboot, or warmstart, one implemented in the software of your CBIOS.

The Difference between Warmboot and Coldboot

Let us turn now to a specific example. Tarbell coldboot hardware selects Drive A, moves the head to track 00, and reads the 80 hex bytes of sector 01—the first sector of the track—into memory at location 0000. It then jumps to location 0000. What happens thereafter thus depends on what was in that sector. Sector 01 of track 00 of a CP/M system disk will contain a short program called the *coldboot loader*.

Warmboot is different. The CP/M standard warmboot jump to 0000—which you can create from the console by holding down the Control key and pressing C, for example—simply vectors you into a specific place in CBIOS. The warmboot code in Tarbell CBIOS selects Drive A, moves the head to track 00 and then reads 42 consecutive sectors (starting at track 00, sector 02) into memory, starting at the first word address (fwa) of CCP. These 42 sectors contain CCP and BDOS.

The coldboot loader reads 51 sectors (starting at track 00, sector 02) into memory, starting at the first word address of CCP. These 51 sectors contain CCP, BDOS, and CBIOS.

Thus the difference between warmboot and coldboot is that coldboot is initiated by hardware and loads CCP, BDOS, and CBIOS and that warmboot is processed entirely by software in CBIOS and necessarily reloads only CCP and BDOS.

The Digital Research specifications for both CP/M 2.2 and CP/M 1.4 calls for warmboot to reload CCP and BDOS, but, as discussed in Chap. 15, some CP/M 2.2 warmboot processors don't reload BDOS and some don't even reload CCP.

Reviewing the Memory Map

In Chap. 7 we constructed a memory map of your CP/M system. Recall that the jump at 0000, the jump at 0005, the file control block at 005C, the record buffer at 0080, and the beginning of all user programs at 0100 are common to all CP/M 1.4 and 2.2 systems, whatever the size of the system memory. Virtually all existing CP/M software assumes that these vectors and buffers exist at these fixed locations. The option to relocate the warmboot origin from 0000 to elsewhere

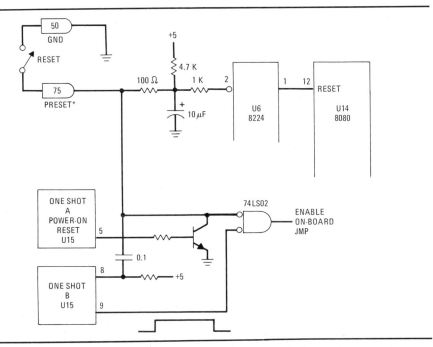

Fig. 12.1 Example of microcomputer reset switch circuit

exists only for those systems that make no use of existing CP/M software. Your memory map will show the actual locations in memory in which your coldboot processor must load CCP, BDOS, and CBIOS.

An Example of RESET Processing

The circuit diagram in Fig. 12.1 shows a typical implementation of a microcomputer reset switch. Anticipating the need for a ROM monitor to assist the system integrator in debugging the coldboot loader, this particular CPU card includes a clever selective reset processing circuit. If you press Reset slowly, you will get a different result from what you will get if you punch it quickly.

If you hold Reset for a little while before letting go, you will get the CPU's *on-board jump*. If you punch Reset quickly, you will activate the Tarbell disk-controller boot circuits. What this amounts to is that by pressing Reset slowly you can invoke a ROM-stored monitor or debugging program instead of activating the coldboot processor. This TEI MCS 8080 CPU board has a little sequencer whose job is to feed a JMP XXYY instruction sequence onto the data bus when you do a slow Reset. The sequencer is enabled when the 556 Timer IC, labeled "One-Shot B," times out. If, and only if, you are still holding Reset closed when One-Shot B times out, you will get the CPU's on-board jump. A ROM monitor can be given control by entering its starting address XXYY into a DIP-switch register on the CPU card.

Coldboot Initiation

If you let go of Reset before One-Shot B times out, then the 8080 will execute whatever instructions it finds on the data bus. What it will find are the instructions being put there—in this case, by the Tarbell disk controller.

The Tarbell disk-controller board has a 32-byte program stored in a ROM of its own. It also has a latch called BOOT that is set directly and immediately by a low level on S-100 bus pin 75, called PRESET*, where the asterisk (*) is used to indicate active-low. When BOOT is set, it enables the 32-byte ROM and disables all other system memories. Since PRESET* will cause the 8080 to set its program counter (PC) to 0000, execution of the 32-byte program listed in Fig. 12.2 will begin at location 0000.

Use of Hardware to Read the First Sector

The first instruction, IN 0FCH, tells the Western Digital 1771 disk controller chip on the Tarbell card to hold low S-100 pin 72, called PRDY, until it has assured itself that the disk's read-head has backed out to track 00. One of the reasons that this single instruction gets so much done is that the 1771 chip itself keeps an eye on the Reset switch. When you let go of Reset, the 1771 chip backs the head out to track 00 by itself. When the disk controller lets go of PRDY, the 8080 asks for the contents of location 0002, and so on. The instructions that follow set HL to 0000, latch the number 01 into the 1771's sector register, and tell the 1771 to read disk data at that sector.

The 1771 pushes the disk into the read-head and starts reading. First it looks for a track identification address mark, and when it finds one, it checks to see that it is indeed looking at track 00. Since the track number and the sector numbers

```
0000    DB FC    IN 0FCH      ;Wait for head HOME
0002    AF       XRA A        ;Set A=00, HL=0000
0003    6F       MOV L,A
0004    67       MOV H,A
0005    3C       INR A        ;Set sector = 01
0006    D3 FA    OUT 0FAH
0008    3E 8C    MVI A,8CH    ;Read command=1000 1100
000A    D3 F8    OUT 0F8H
000C    DB FC    IN 0FCH      ;Wait for data; read status
000E    B7       ORA A        ;To set flags
000F    F2       JP 0019H     ;If 128 bytes read
0010    19 00
0012    DB FB    IN 0FBH      ;Read the data byte
0014    77       MOV M,A      ;Store data in memory
0015    23       INX H        ;Advance memory address
0016    C3       JMP 000CH    ;Loop for 128 bytes
0017    0C 00
0019    DB F8    IN 0F8H      ;Read status
001B    B7       ORA A
001C    CA       JZ 007DH     ;If no read errors
001D    7D 00
001F    76       HLT
```

Fig. 12.2 *A bootloader program used to start CP/M*

are written in each sector on the disk, the 1771 simply reads identification records until it finds the sector we've asked for.

If the track number on the disk doesn't match the track requested—in our case, the track requested was set to 00 by Reset—then the 1771 sets an error bit in its status word and discontinues the search. The 1771 also keeps an eye on that little "index hole" that is going round and round in there. If that little hole goes around more than twice while the 1771 is looking for our sector, it will set "Record Not Found" in its status word and stop looking for our sector.

Meanwhile, back at the S-100 bus, you will find that all the while this search has been going on, the disk controller has been holding its foot on the 8080 by keeping PRDY low. When the 1771 finds our sector, it will first read a data byte and store it in its own data register; then it will set status on the data bus before it lets go of PRDY. As soon as PRDY is released, the 8080 executes instruction IN 0FCH. This brings disk status into the A-register. If the high-order bit is set, then we issue IN 0FBH to bring the data byte into the CPU. We store the byte in RAM, advance HL, and loop back for another byte.

When the high-order status bit indicates that 128 bytes have been read, we exit the loop and reread the status. If all bits are zero, we have a good read. We jump to 007D instead of directly to 0000 because if we jumped directly to 0000 we would just re-execute the ROM boot. The reason is that the latch called *BOOT* is still latched. The way we unlatch it is to get address bit A5 set high. The jump to 007D does just that. The thing that we have just brought into RAM should be the Tarbell coldboot loader, called *SBOOT*. If you look at location 007D in SBOOT, you will find, as you would expect, the instruction JMP 0000. SBOOT is now loaded and has been given control.

Use of Software to Load the CP/M Resident

If this is a 48k Tarbell system, SBOOT will read sector 02 and store it at location A500—the first word address of CCP. SBOOT will continue reading the disk and writing into memory until it has read and loaded 51 sectors. Starting at track 00, sector 02, it will have read through track 01, sector 26 (decimal). SBOOT will have loaded CCP at A500, BDOS at AD00, and CBIOS at BA00. The last thing that SBOOT does is to jump to the first byte of CBIOS at BA00.

Control Taken Over by the Resident

The CBIOS coldboot code at BA00 reaches back and stores instruction JMP BA03 into location 0000 and instruction JMP AD06 into location 0005. The jump at 0000 is a vector into warmboot code in CBIOS. The jump at 0005 is a vector into the system manager, BDOS. Standard CP/M applications programs do all of their input and output by means of the instruction sequence

```
LXI     D,param
MVI     C,function code
CALL    0005
```

The vector at 0005 is one of the most important standard features of CP/M. All CP/M applications programs are coded to load and begin at 0100H, and all assume that BDOS is accessible via the linkage provided by the vector at 0005.

Coldboot code in Tarbell CBIOS puts out a message to the console asking for the number of disk drives available. What it really wants to know is if you are running a one-drive system because it contains a special code to assist you in copying disk-to-disk on this system. CP/M 1.4 can handle up to four disk drives; CP/M 2.2, up to 16 disk drives. CBIOS saves your answer, selects Drive A by putting 00 into the C-register, and then jumps directly to the first byte of CCP.

CCP issues the sequence

```
MVI     C,0D
CALL    0005
```

This *initialize function* causes BDOS to scan the directory of the disk in Drive A and build in memory a bit-map of the record blocks that are in use on this disk. This operation logs in the disk in Drive A.

While scanning the directory, BDOS function 0D also watches for *submit files*. If a submit file is present, BDOS returns a *nonzero* value in the A-register. If no submit file exists, CCP finally prints a console prompt character. You are up and running.

Differences between Systems

Many of the coldboot process details in your own system may be different from those described here, but the end result must be identical to the result developed by the process described. With the required result in mind, you will be better equipped to study the coldboot documentation provided with your own system.

Summary

An important observation to be drawn from a study of the coldboot process is that a large number of details have to be correctly arranged before the first CCP prompt character can appear on your console. A system that is able to boot up cannot have a lot of things wrong with it. When trouble appears, you will save time and trouble by thinking patiently and carefully about your program and about your operating procedure before looking for a hardware explanation. Improper log-in of a disk is a common procedural error. In the next chapter, we will further explore the implications of the CP/M disk log-in procedure.

CHAPTER 13

Logging In and Swapping Out

ALWAYS INITIALIZE A CP/M system after swapping disks. There are three ways to do so:

1. Do a coldboot by hitting Reset
2. Do a warmboot by using console Control-C or a programmed jump to 0000
3. Do a programmed BDOS function 0D

Always close the files on an output disk before removing it. Always close all output files before initializing the system.

The Initialize Function

The essential ingredient in each of these three options is the BDOS function 0D. This function causes BDOS to clear all RBR tables, to mark all disks logged out, and to log in the disk in Drive A. Under CP/M 2.2, there exists a fourth alternative in the form of a BDOS function that selectively logs out the drive whose disk is to be swapped.

Call DDT with the command

DDT

Put DDT into assembler-mode with the command

A100

and type the following program:

> *MVI C,0D*
> *CALL 5*
> *RET*

Get out of assembler-mode with an extra carriage return, that is, an empty line at the end. Now list your program with the command

> *L100*

The DDT listing should be

> *0100   MVI C,0D*
> *0102   CALL 0005*
> *0105   RET*

The code following location 0105 is immaterial. Get out of DDT with G0 or Control-C, and save the program with the command

> *SAVE 1 BDOSF0D.COM*

Testing the Initialize Function

Put a disk into drive B and log it in with the command

> *B:*

Go back to drive A with the command

> *A:*

Use the command

> *STAT*

to show that there are two disks logged in. Now issue a BDOS function 0D by calling your program with the command

> *BDOSF0D*

The command

> *STAT*

should now reveal that only one disk is logged in.

Allocation Tables

At 0BFA locations past the first word of any CP/M 1.4 BDOS, there is the first of four 32-byte tables called *Allocation Tables* or *Record Block Reservation* (RBR) tables. CP/M 1.4 supports up to four disk drives, meaning that there are four allocation tables. Under CP/M 2.2, there can be up to sixteen disk RBR tables appearing in CBIOS. The program developed in Chap. 10, called RBRDIS, will display any allocation table under either CP/M 1.4 or CP/M 2.2 by calling it with a command of the form

> *RBRDIS d:*

where d: gives the name of the disk drive whose RBR is to be displayed.

The reserve block, also called the *reservation block* or *record block*, is the smallest amount of disk space that can be reserved. For example, on the CP/M standard 8-inch single-density disk, the reserve block consists of eight CP/M sectors. A CP/M sector is always 128 bytes.

The first reservable block on a standard single-density CP/M disk begins at track 02, sector 01, the first sector of track two. From that point to the end of the disk there are 75 tracks containing 26 CP/M sectors each. The total space to be divided into reserve blocks is 1950 CP/M sectors. Dividing this figure by eight, we find that we have 243.75 reserve blocks. Since the fractional block of six sectors is not used, this disk can hold 243 reserve blocks. In hexadecimal, the reserve blocks on this standard single-density disk are named 00 through F2.

Disk Log-In

When CBIOS jumps to CCP following either a coldboot or a warmboot, CCP calls BDOS with function code 0D, the initialize function, which causes BDOS to clear all allocation tables and then scan all directory entries on the disk in drive A. If byte 00 of a directory entry is not E5, which indicates an empty entry, then the record block names in bytes 10 through 1F of the directory entry are used as ordinals to set reservation bits in Drive A's RBR table. BDOS then sets the low-order bit of the log-in vector to indicate that the disk in Drive A is logged in.

The Log-In Vector

For four drives, A, B, C, and D, the bits in the log-in vector are arranged in the order

> *xxxxdcba*

You can read the log-in vector with a BDOS function sequence such as

```
MVI   C, 18H
CALL  0005
ANI   02H     ;HL=AB=log-in vector
JNZ   _____   ;If Drive 'B' logged in
```

Log-Out Function

A BDOS function to clear bits in the log-in vector selectively is available under CP/M 2.2. This function can be used to log out a drive selectively and thereby avoid the necessity of closing all output files on all drives when a disk in any drive is swapped. It is really only the swapped drive that needs to be logged out. Under CP/M 1.4, however, there is no selective log-out; there is only function 0D.

A Typical Directory Entry

The 243 reserve blocks of the standard single-density CP/M disk are numbered 00 through F2. Reserve blocks 00 and 01 on this disk are always reserved for the directory. Reserve block 02 is the first block that can be reserved by the user. The disk dump reproduced in Fig. 13.1 exhibits a typical directory entry that might appear on a standard CP/M disk. Bytes 01 through 08 represent the file name PIP. The three character filetype COM appears in bytes 09, 0A, and 0B. The hex value 37 in byte 0F tells us that PIP is 37 hex, or 55 decimal, CP/M sectors in total size. Beginning at byte 10 and running through byte 16, we see the names of the reserve blocks occupied by the copy of PIP.COM. Since 55 divided by eight is 6.895, we would expect PIP to occupy seven reserve blocks, as indeed it does. The hex value 37 in byte 0F implies that the end-of-information on this file is at the end of the seventh sector of reserve block 08.

Reading Always Possible

Suppose that we remove from Drive A the disk containing this copy of PIP.COM and replace it with a different disk, but one that also contains a copy of the file PIP.COM. On this new disk, suppose that PIP.COM is not at reserve block 02, but elsewhere. If we now call PIP with the CCP command

> PIP

will CCP be able to find PIP on the disk? When CCP opens the file PIP.COM by calling BDOS, BDOS will search the directory on the disk now present, and thus CCP will correctly load PIP into memory. PIP will issue a prompt (*) to let you know it is ready for your next command. Suppose now that you place into Drive B a disk that contains a copy of some file you want, and suppose that to copy this file to the disk in Drive A, you issue the command

> *MYFILE.ASM=B:SUBLIB.ASM

Writing Not Always Possible

When PIP goes to work on this copy operation, it may overwrite occupied blocks of the disk in Drive A. If you remember the exercise performed in Chap.

	0	1	2	3	4	5	6	7	8	9	A	B	C	D	E	F
0	00	50	49	50	20	20	20	20	20	43	4F	4D	00	00	00	37
1	02	03	04	05	06	07	08	00	00	00	00	00	00	00	00	00

Fig. 13.1 *Example of directory entry for the file PIP.COM*

10, the bits in the Drive A RBR correspond at this moment to those of the removed disk. When BDOS goes to that RBR to find space for MYFILE.ASM, it will be examining an invalid table. Since it could easily arrive at a mistaken conclusion, overwrite of current files on the disk in Drive A may result.

Directory Checksum

CP/M goes to some pains to try to help you avoid this problem. When it logs in a disk, it separately checksums each sector of the directory on that disk. Later, it uses these checksums to try to detect when you switch disks in order to prevent you from writing on a disk that is not logged in. If BDOS detects that you have switched disks, you will get a warning message

BDOS ERR ON A: R/O

If BDOS doesn't detect the switch, you will be in a mess. The simplest safeguard is to do a warmboot every time you switch a disk. If you plan only to read, then the disk doesn't have to be logged in. If you can't do a warmboot, then you must use BDOS function 0D or BDOS function 25H (37 decimal) after you switch a disk and before you write on it. BDOS function 0D is available, for example, as the CBASIC statement INITIALIZE.

Keeping Aware of Disks Logged In

STAT watches the log-in vector. On a two-drive system, the command

STAT

responds with

A: R/W, SPACE: 89K
B: R/W, SPACE: 143K

for example, when both drives are logged in, but with

A: R/W, SPACE 88K

for example, when only one drive is logged in.

Any program that ends up jumping to 0000, as many programs do, will thereby invoke a warmstart, which will invoke a BDOS initialize function, which, in turn, will clear all allocations and log in the disk in Drive A.

In response to

STAT

you will get one line displayed because even if the last command was

PIP B:ED.COM=ED.COM

only one disk will be logged in because PIP is one of those programs that end by jumping to 0000.

The one-line STAT response

A: R/W, SPACE 88K

tells us that Drive A is logged in and all other drives logged out. To be logged out is a safe state, safer than to be logged in. If Drive B is logged out and we put a disk into it and then write on the disk, the space will be allocated correctly because BDOS will log in the disk just before writing on it. The fresh log-in will develop an accurate RBR from the RBT in the directory on the disk.

It is when a drive is logged in that we must be careful. Since Drive A is almost always logged in, we must be extra careful about swapping disks in and out of Drive A. While a disk is logged in, BDOS will use the RBR in memory to find unreserved blocks for your new files as you write them.

Necessity of Closing Files

It is important to understand that merely writing information correctly at the places BDOS has correctly made available on a disk in no way secures permanent reservation of that space. Correctly allocated disk space is reserved securely *only when* the file is closed. When you close a file, the image of the file's directory entry residing in the file control block is copied into the directory on the disk, thus assuring its permanence.

File extents further confuse the issue. If you write a large file of, for example, 20k bytes on a CP/M standard single-density disk and then exit the program without closing the file, the first 16k will have been closed by BDOS and therefore correctly reserved, but the tail end of the file will not be represented in the RBT on the disk and will therefore not be permanently reserved.

Any applications program specifically written for CP/M, such as Microsoft BASIC, is naturally going to go to some effort to assure that all output files are closed before ending. (In Chap. 1, however, we exhibited a way to exit Microsoft BASIC without closing files. That one example should serve to illustrate that "automatic" operations do not negate the value of understanding fundamentals.)

Threaded and Unthreaded Files

Some disk operating systems "thread" or "chain" their files, that is, they place in each sector or block of the file a pointer giving the disk location of the next sector or block of the file. This kind of file can be read even if it isn't entirely represented in the systems's disk directory. All you have to do is pick up the beginning of the thread and then follow it on the disk to the end of the file.

CP/M files, however, are not threaded. Unless you close a CP/M file, there is no way to determine where all blocks of the file are located on the disk even if you know the location of the first sector. The CP/M file structure is based on pure random disk access. Successful file operations always depend on current information being present in the disk directory.

Reliability of Checksum

The checksum that BDOS makes for each sector of the directory is an eight-bit checksum. An eight-bit quantity can take on exactly 256 different values. Whenever you switch disks without initializing or otherwise logging out the drive, you have exactly one chance in 256 of having the switch go undetected. Most of the time, BDOS will catch it and respond

BDOS ERR ON x: R/O

When this response appears, it is possible but improbable that you have a hardware problem. On the other hand, it is possible and highly probable that you have switched disks without initializing.

Even more trouble is caused by the one time in 256 when you switch disks and appear to get away with it. When BDOS doesn't detect the switch, it is possible and probable that space on the new disk already in use will be overwritten.

We might ask, "If BDOS knows that a disk has been swapped, why doesn't it go ahead and log in the new disk?" That sounds like a good idea, and it is; moreover, that's exactly what BDOS does. But there is a problem. BDOS doesn't know what files, if any, you have open. An open file has a valid directory entry only in the file control block. As you write the file, reservation bits are set in the RBR (somewhere in the CP/M resident), and corresponding reservation block bytes or words are set in the FCB (somewhere in your program).

When BDOS detects that you've swapped disks without initializing, it knows that there is very little it can be sure of. For example, since it has no record of what files, if any, you have open, it knows that if it allows your program to continue running, it is possible for a file to be closed that was actually opened on the previous disk. The only thing needed for a successful closing on the new disk is for the file name to exist in the directory of the new disk. It is then possible for you to have two directory entries on the new disk pointing to the same reservation blocks. The varieties of chaos are infinite, and we could continue postulating possibilities indefinitely. Nevertheless, when BDOS puts out its diagnostic message and takes action, there is only a small probability of the situation being confounded. BDOS gives you a warmboot.

One of the more troublesome aspects of this problem is that you can violate the rules and not only appear to get away with it but actually do so. CP/M 1.3 doesn't have the checksum feature. As a result, under 1.3 you always appear to get away with swapping without initializing. The real problem, in a sense, is that this does not cause trouble every time. If it did so every time, it might not take new users so long to catch on to the importance of initializing after every swap.

The checksum feature we now have in CP/M is not fail-safe, but it has the advantage of device independence. It will work most of the time, and with a little assistance based on an understanding of the fundamentals, it will work all of the time.

A fail-safe system would not be slower; it would be faster. The problem is that it would be device-dependent. A fail-safe system requires a latch on the controller that is set by the computer, cleared by the drive, and read by the computer. The computer sets the latch when logging in the disk. The drive clears the latch whenever the disk is dismounted. Unfortunately, such a latch is not standard.

Summary

Once you learn to keep aware of which disks are logged in, and you understand that a file has not really been written until it has been closed, two major sources of CP/M confusion will have been removed, and the incidence of mysterious disk problems will be considerably reduced.

14

Higher Capacity Disks

C *P/M 1 WAS* written for the Intel 8080 with the IBM 3740 single-density disk in mind. That disk can hold, roughly speaking, a quarter of a million characters. If you divide that amount of storage space into 250 compartments called *record blocks*, each block will hold about 1000 characters—a compellingly convenient arrangement for the eight-bit 8080. Since an eight-bit byte can take on exactly 256 different values, it can distinguish, or point to, any one of 250 record blocks.

Disk Division

CP/M 1.4 divides the single-density disk into 243 record blocks, each of which can hold 1024 bytes, called 1K. Each eight-bit byte can hold one character or any other eight-bit value. This arrangement is, and will remain, important because it is the standard format used for the distribution of CP/M software.

Higher capacity disks have upset this convenient arrangement, among them double-density and double-sided/double-density disks, "Winchesters," and also the 2315 and 5440 cartridge-type disks. Consider, for example, the Western Dynex 6222 top-loading 5440 cartridge type disk drive. It includes a fixed disk that holds five million characters and a removable cartridge that holds another five million characters. If we were to divide a five-million character storage space into only 250 compartments, each would hold 20,000 characters. Twenty thousand characters is not a convenient size for a reservation block. Experience has shown that even 1000-character blocks are sometimes too big. Blocks twenty times bigger would leave far too much space unused since too many blocks would be reserved for, and occupied by, one small file that would actually require only a fraction of the space reserved.

Record Block Reservation Words

The fundamental difference between CP/M 1.4 and CP/M 2.2 is that CP/M 2.2 has the ability to divide a disk into more than 256 parts. CP/M 1.4 provides for eight-bit record block names called *record block reservation bytes*, whereas CP/M 2.2 provides for 16-bit record block names, called *record block reservation words*. With a 16-bit word, we can give a unique name to as many as 65,536 reservation blocks.

Differences between BDOS and CBIOS

Under CP/M 1.4, all disk division parameters and reservation tables are stored in BDOS. In this we find a major structural difference between CP/M 1.4 and CP/M 2.2. Under CP/M 2.2, all disk division parameters and reservation tables are located in CBIOS, which is where they really belong. This difference has some significance for our present purpose, because CBIOS, unlike BDOS for which you may never see source code, is usually available in source code form. The reason is that the CBIOS portion of your CP/M system has to be provided by the system integrator; it doesn't come with the material received from Digital Research.

Hewlett-Packard, Heath-Zenith, Xerox Data Systems, Murrow Designs, Tarbell Electronics, Digital Microsystems, Burns & Foster, your local computer store—these are just a few examples of system integrators. System integrators who deliver full-service "turn-key" systems usually do not provide CBIOS source code to the final user. Whether or not you need CBIOS source code depends on whether you intend to handle your own system modifications. If your vendor is to provide all needed CBIOS modifications, you will not need CBIOS source code.

Summary

Up to 16 disks, each of which may hold up to 8,388,608 bytes ($512 \times 16 \times 1024$) can be managed by the 16-bit address scheme used by CP/M 2.2. In other words, CP/M 2.2 can manage somewhat over 128 megabytes of disk storage. The manner in which the disk is divided for address purposes is decided by your system integrator and the resulting specification is built into your CBIOS.

CHAPTER 15

Booting
the CP/M 2.2

ONCE WE DEPART from the standard 8-inch single-density CP/M disk, there is no standard. Higher capacity disks are usually not intended to be transportable from one CP/M system to another. Higher capacity removable media, such as the 5440 type cartridge, can ordinarily be exchanged only between systems assembled by the same system integrator. For example, the CBIOS provided by KONAN for their KNX-500 Western Dynex controller uses a reservation block size different from that of the CBIOS provided by Burns & Foster for the CAMEO DC500 Western Dynex controller. The 5440 disk packs are physically exchangeable between the two systems, but they are logically incompatible.

Distribution of CP/M Software

All CP/M systems should provide and retain the ability to read and write standard 8-inch single-density *distribution format disks*. You can certainly create and use systems without this capability, but you may have cut yourself off from easy access to much of the vast library of CP/M software whose existence represents one of the main reasons for using CP/M in the first place.

Higher capacity disks are important in expanding CP/M to a broader range of applications, but their importance is in a sense local rather than global. A higher capacity disk should be optimized for local performance, with little consideration given to making the disk transportable. Indeed, since many of the new higher capacity disks are not dismountable, no question of transportability exists.

Nondismountable Media

When we come to nondismountable media, the CP/M development that we have been following takes a curious turn. One might expect that to a large measure the CP/M disk structure would lose significance when compared to the structure of nondismountable media. Some of it does. Certainly there is no reason to checksum the directory of a nondismountable disk, but the superfluity of this feature was anticipated, and CP/M 2.2 permits it to be selectively disabled. A few years ago it made sense to keep the directory of a fixed disk in core memory since the ferrite-core memory was as permanent across power-outs as the disk itself. Today's volatile semiconductor memory requires that all disk directories be kept on the disk itself; the CP/M disk structure is still valid and even appropriate on the latest fixed Winchesters.

Two–Step Start–Up

The CBIOS for a CP/M 2.2 system that includes significantly higher capacity disks will typically be too large to fit into the six sectors reserved for CBIOS in the system space of a standard CP/M single-density disk. In a situation such as this, the system can be started by a two-step procedure. First, a CP/M system configured for only single-density, or other lower capacity disk, is coldstarted, and then a program executable as a normal transient command from that disk is called to load the higher capacity system. In other words, the higher capacity system is designed with the assumptions that it will be installed in a computer that has a lower capacity floppy-disk system already running and that the floppy-disk controller or other original coldstart sequencer will continue to be responsible for all coldstarts.

Creating a CP/M Loader

The CP/M relocation utility program—CPM.COM, or MOVCPM.COM— can provide essential ingredients for the construction of a system loader permitting installation of virtually any size CBIOS. The procedure is best illustrated by a specific example.

Our chosen system consists of a Western Dynex 6222 ten-megabyte 5440 cartridge type disk drive—five megabytes fixed, five megabytes removable— with a Cameo controller and two Shugart 801R floppy-disk drives with a Tarbell single-density floppy-disk controller. Our chosen computer has 64k of RAM.

The basic idea is to make room for the expanded CBIOS by moving CCP and BDOS down in memory. The word *down* refers to lower memory location values. We do this by telling CPM.COM to create a CP/M resident for a 62k memory with the command

CPM 62 *

and then we save this resident image with the command

SAVE 34 MYCPM.COM

Our expanded CBIOS will have been assembled with its origin at F200, and hence we have the Intel format hex file CBIOS.HEX on disk. We merge this CBIOS into our CP/M resident image by using DDT as follows:

DDT MYCPM.COM

ICBIOS.HEX
R2D80

When DDT adds the value 2D80 to F200, which is the starting address for our CBIOS, it will load the first byte of CBIOS into location 1F80, the correct starting location for CBIOS in the CP/M resident image.

The CP/M resident image now in memory starting at location 0980 is our Dynex system. All we have to do to start the Dynex system is move this image to the top of memory, set the vectors at 0000 and 0005, and jump to the first byte of CCP. A short program will handle the move, and the standard coldstart code in CBIOS will do the rest.

First, get out of DDT with Control-C or G0, and then save the resident image with the command

SAVE 45 CPM62.COM

A program to move the resident image to its actual operating location is listed in Fig. 15.1. If this source code file is created under the name CPMLGO.ASM, assembly will create the file CPMLGO.HEX. We can then use DDT to merge this image moving program, CPMLGO, with our CP/M image.

Reload the CP/M image under DDT with the command

DDT CPM62.COM

Merge CPMLGO and the CP/M image with the DDT commands

ICPMLGO.HEX
R

Get out of DDT with Control-C or G0, and then save the load-and-go program with the command

SAVE 45 CPMLGO.COM

The command

CPMLGO

will now start the Dynex system.

The Burns & Foster CBIOS is arranged to warmboot off the Dynex disk. To copy the CP/M resident image on the system track of either the fixed

```
                    ;File:   CPMLGO.ASM
                    ;Edit date:     81/09/11.
                    ;
                    ;       CPMLGO - CP/M Load and Go.
                    ;       The CP/M resident image is assumed to be at 0980H.
                    ;
0980 =              IMAGE   EQU     0980H               ;Image fwa
2F80 =              SIZE    EQU     3000H-80H           ;Image size
                    ;
0100                        ORG     0100H
                    ;
0100 313301  LGO:          LXI     SP,STACK
0103 3A8209               LDA     IMAGE+2             ;Set DE=CCP fwa
0106 D603                 SUI     3
0108 57                   MOV     D,A
0109 1E00                 MVI     E,0
010B 210016               LXI     H,1600H             ;Set HL=CBIOS fwa
010E 19                   DAD     D
010F 221C01               SHLD    CBOOT
                    ;
0112 218009               LXI     H,IMAGE             ;Source
0115 0180D0               LXI     B,-SIZE             ;-byte count
0118 CD1E01               CALL    MMV                 ;Move image
                    ;
011B C30000               JMP     0000                ;Go to CBIOS Coldboot
011C =       CBOOT        EQU     $-2
                    ;
                    ;       MMV - Memory Move.
                    ;       Entry   HL = Source fwa
                    ;               DE = Destination fwa
                    ;               BC = - byte count
                    ;
011E 7E12     MMV:         MOV     A,M ! STAX D
0120 13230C               INX     D ! INX H ! INR C
0123 C21E01               JNZ     MMV
0126 04C21E01C9           INR     B ! JNZ MMV ! RET
                    ;
012B                      DS      8
0133          STACK:      DS      0
```

Fig. 15.1 *Assembly listing for CPMLGO*

or removable disk, Burns & Foster provide a utility similar to SYSGEN, called DSKGEN. DSKGEN expects to read the CP/M image from a file named DSKGEN.SYS. We therefore create this file with the command

PIP DSKGEN.SYS=CPM62.COM

and we then call DSKGEN to transfer the CP/M image to the system track. Since each track of this particular Dynex disk can hold 12k, there is more than enough space to hold this particular 9k CP/M resident even though it is much too big for the 6.5k of space available on two tracks of a standard single-density floppy disk.

The Cameo controller provides no coldstart facility such as that found on the Tarbell floppy-disk controller. To coldstart directly from the Dynex disk, we could install a system loader in ROM to be invoked through, for example, a CPU on-board jump. But coldstart from floppy disk is sufficient in most cases because, in a well-running system, coldstart typically occurs only once a day. Since warmstart, on the other hand, can occur frequently, Burns & Foster have arranged for their Dynex CBIOS to warmstart off the Dynex disk rather than the floppy disk. If we had CBIOS warmstart off the floppy disk, we would most likely have to keep the floppy disk mounted at all times. It's more convenient to warmstart the Dynex system from the Dynex drive and to run with the floppies loaded only while they are actually being used.

Differences in Reloading BDOS and CCP

The warmstart code in CBIOS can be simplified to reload CCP only, rather than both CCP and BDOS. Warmstart in Tarbell 2.2 and Burns & Foster 2.2 reloads all of CCP plus the first sector of BDOS. This reloading is actually sufficient even though the Digital Research specification calls for warmstart to reload both CCP and BDOS. All standard CP/M user programs must retain BDOS intact. The only reason for reloading the first sector of BDOS is to restore the first six bytes of BDOS, which are, in effect, part of CCP.

If your system includes a background print-file-spooling utility loaded below CCP, warmstart doesn't have to reload anything at all, its only function being to restore the vector at 0005, followed by a jump to CCP. The reason for this is that in order to protect itself from being overwritten, the spooling utility will change the vector at 0005 to point to its own first byte. This change actually does two things. It allows the spooling utility to intercept BDOS calls, while at the same time it marks its own first word address as the upper limit of user-alterable memory. A side effect of this arrangement is that DDT, when loaded, no longer overlays CCP.

Summary

As may be implied from this discussion of a CP/M 2.2 start-up, CP/M 2.2 has many options. There will be as many start-up procedures as there are system integrators, but as we emphasized earlier, all CP/M start-up processors must create the same end result. The CP/M resident must be loaded into the upper portion of memory, the vectors at 0000 and 0005 must be created, and the console command processor must be given control.

16

Batch Processing

*R*EPETITIVE SEQUENCES OF commands can be saved in a text file and submitted to CP/M for processing when needed. This batch-processing facility is made available through the SUBMIT utility program described in the Digital Research manual, "An Introduction to CP/M Features and Facilities" (page 28). Read the Digital Research description of SUBMIT before starting the following exercise.

Warmstart to Initiate the Process

Whenever BDOS processes function 0D, the initialize function, it watches for a file named $$$.SUB on the disk in Drive A. If such a file is present, BDOS returns a nonzero value in the A-register. When entered at its first word address, as it is after a warmboot, CCP issues BDOS function 0D and will then process the $$$.SUB file if it is present.

Creating $$$.SUB

In practice, we use the utility program SUBMIT.COM to create the file $$$.SUB, but in this exercise we will create this file "by hand." We will first make a slight alteration of our random access test program, RANDOMEX.
Load RANDOMEX.COM under DDT with the command

DDT RANDOMEX.COM

Near the beginning of the program, change the instruction LXI D,DMA to LXI D,DMA−1 by opening location 0104 for modification with the DDT command

S104

In response to

0104 88

type 87 and then press carriage return. Press the space bar and then another carriage return to end the S command. This modification will cause the text character count to appear in the first byte of each text record written.

In the subroutine RRT, change the program so that it will store 00 at the end of the record text instead of $. Use the DDT command

S394

to open location 0394 for modification. Then, in response to

0394 24

type 00 followed by carriage return. Now press the space bar and another carriage return to end the S command. Get out of DDT with Control-C, and save the modified program with the command.

SAVE 4 SUBTEST.COM

Our new program, SUBTEST, is identical to RANDOMEX except that it terminates text lines with 00 instead of $ and that it provides the text character count in the first byte of each text record.

Verify the availability of the program DUMP.COM with the command

DIR DUMP.*

This utility is provided with CP/M by Digital Research, and its source code is listed and described in the Digital Research manual, "CP/M 2.2 Interface Guide" (page 34).

Erase any existing TESTFILE.TMP with the command

ERA TESTFILE.TMP

Call the new program with the command

SUBTEST

Write into record number 0 the text

DIR *.ASM

Write into record number 1 the text

DIR *.BAK

Write into record number 2 the text

*DIR *.COM*

Then get out of SUBTEST with Control-C.

We have written the file named TESTFILE.TMP. The file contains three CP/M records, each having one control statement or command. The order of the control statements, as written, is

*DIR *.ASM*
*DIR *.BAK*
*DIR *.COM*

Imitating SUBMIT

To submit these control statements to CCP for batch processing, copy TESTFILE.TMP to $$$.SUB with the command

PIP $$$.SUB=TESTFILE.TMP

When PIP completes this copy operation, $$$.SUB will have been created, and the warmboot invoked by PIP, when it jumps to 0000, will shift CCP into batch command processing mode. Verify that the order in which the commands are processed is inverse to the order in which the commands appear in the file.

Using SUBMIT Itself

Call the editor with the command

ED TEST.SUB

and create the file TEST.SUB containing these three text lines:

*DIR *.COM*
*DIR *.BAK*
*DIR *.ASM*

End the edit session with the E command, and then submit these control statements with the command

SUBMIT TEST

Verify that the result obtained is the same as the result we obtained after creating $$$.SUB from TESTFILE.TMP via PIP.

Structure of $$$.SUB

Utility program SUBMIT reads the file TEST.SUB and writes one control statement per CP/M record into the file named $$$.SUB, the last control statement in TEST.SUB being written to the first record of $$$.SUB. The order of control statements is inverted to allow CCP to read sequential control statements by simply reading the last record of $$$.SUB and then chopping that record off the end of the file by decrementing the file's record count in the FCB before closing the file. Each time CCP opens $$$.SUB, the file is one record shorter. When the file reaches zero length, CCP deletes $$$.SUB.

Parameter Substitution

Edit the file TEST.SUB by calling the editor with the command

> *ED TEST.SUB*

Do not bring existing text from the file into the text buffer, but put the editor into input-mode with the i command instead. Then type in the command line

> *DUMP $1.SUB*

followed by carriage return. Get out of input mode with Control-Z, and end the edit session with the E command. To verify that the editor has appended all existing text from the file to this new command, display the file with the command

> *TYPE TEST.SUB*

The file should now contain the commands

> *DUMP $1.SUB*
> *DIR *.COM*
> *DIR *.BAK*
> *DIR *.ASM*

Submit this batch of control statements with the command

> *SUBMIT TEST $$$*

SUBMIT will substitute $$$ for $1 in the command DUMP $1.SUB and write the command into the file $$$.SUB in the form

> *DUMP $$$.SUB*

When DUMP executes, stop display scrolling with Control-S, and verify that the last command of the sequence

> *DIR *.ASM*

occupies the first record of the file $$$.SUB. The first record will, of course, contribute the last control statement to the batch sequence.

Parameter substitution, and the XSUB function, extend the SUBMIT utility to applications beyond the batch processing of fixed batches of control statements.

XSUB

The XSUB function is described in the Digital Research manual, "CP/M 2 User's Guide" (page 11).

XSUB is designed to load itself into memory just below CCP by computing its load location from the contents of memory location 0006, the address portion of the vector at 0005. It then changes the vector at 0005 to point to itself so that it can intercept BDOS functions and watch for BDOS function 10, the console line input function.

If a print-file-spooling utility is already present in memory just below CCP, it will have modified the vector at 0005 so that it can intercept the same BDOS functions. At best, XSUB will then misjudge its proper load location in memory and use 2k more memory than necessary in its attempt to locate itself below what it believes to be CCP. Test simultaneous spooling and XSUB processing before attempting to work under this arrangement.

Create the file $$$.SUB by using the command

REN $$$.SUB=TESTFILE.TMP

This built-in CCP command does not invoke a warmboot. Now call the extended submit processor with the command

XSUB

and verify that XSUB reads commands from $$$.SUB and delivers them to CCP just as if they had been typed at the console. XSUB is intercepting the BDOS functions 10 issued by CCP itself. XSUB reads the file $$$.SUB last-record-first, using the same file-truncating technique used by CCP.

Find your source file HELLO.ASM and copy it with the command

PIP YHELLO.ASM=HELLO.ASM

Call the editor with the command

ED YHELLO.ASM

Bring in the entire file with the #A command, and then use the edit command

FMVI↑Z0LT

to position the text pointer to the first source instruction in the program, that is, the instruction

MVI C,9

Go into input-mode with i followed by carriage return, and insert the instruction

LXI SP,STACK

as the new first instruction of the program. Get out of input-mode with Control-Z and move the text pointer to the end of the program with the −B command. Go back into input-mode with i and add these three new text lines to the end of the program:

> *DS 65*
> *DS 20 ;Room for 10 pushes*
> *STACK   EQU $*

Get out of input-mode with Control-Z, and end the edit session with the E command.

Assemble YHELLO with the command

> *ASM YHELLO*

If there are any assembly errors, compare your assembly listing with the listing of YHELLO in Fig. 16.1. Edit your program, if necessary, and reassemble. When you have an error-free assembly, create YHELLO.COM with the command

> *LOAD YHELLO*

```
                    ;File:   HELLO.ASM
                    ;
     0100                        ORG     0100H
                    ;
     0100 319E01                 LXI     SP,STACK
     0103 0E09                   MVI     C,9        ;Ask for name
     0105 113001                 LXI     D,ASK
     0108 CD0500                 CALL    5
                    ;
     010B 0E0A                   MVI     C,10            ;Read the name
     010D 114801                 LXI     D,BUF
     0110 CD0500                 CALL    5
                    ;
                    ;   Put a space between "Hi" and the person's name.
                    ;
     0113 214801                 LXI     H,BUF
     0116 3620                    MVI     M,20H      ;ASCII space, or blank
     0118 23                     INX     H
     0119 5E                     MOV     E,M        ;Get number of characters in answer
     011A 3620                    MVI     M,20H
     011C 1600                    MVI     D,0
     011E 23                     INX     H
     011F 19                     DAD     D
     0120 3621                    MVI     M,'!'
     0122 23                     INX     H
     0123 3624                    MVI     M,'$'
                    ;
     0125 0E09                   MVI     C,9        ;Say "Hi"
     0127 114401                 LXI     D,ANS
     012A CD0500                 CALL    5
                    ;
     012D C30000                 JMP     0000       ;Return to CCP
                    ;
     0130 5768617420ASK:         DB   'What is your name? $'
     0144 0D0A4869  ANS:         DB   0DH,0AH,'Hi'
     0148 41        BUF:         DB   65     ;Buffer size is 65 characters
     0149                        DS      65
     018A                        DS      20     ;Room for 10 pushes
     019E =         STACK        EQU     $
```

Fig. 16.1 *Assembly listing for YHELLO (YHELLO is HELLO modified to provide its own stack area)*

Test this new program by calling it with the command

>*YHELLO*

Its operation should be identical to the operation of HELLO. The original program of HELLO uses CCP's push-down stack when called by CCP or a stack at 0100 when executed under DDT.

The stack set up by CCP when it uses the instruction

>*CALL 0100*

to start a user program has room for eight *pushes*. This CALL instruction uses one of those eight words, leaving room for seven pushes. When HELLO uses the instruction

>*CALL 0005*

to process BDOS function 10, this call uses another stack space, leaving room for six pushes. If this call truly went directly to BDOS, there would be no problem because BDOS has a stack of its own. But if function 10 should be intercepted by XSUB, we are in for deep trouble because XSUB pushes into the user's stack seven times. If that user happens to be HELLO, which is itself using CCP's stack, the address portion of a JMP instruction in CCP will be overwritten by data pushed on the stack by XSUB, and the system will crash.

Call the program

>*SUBTEST*

and write into record 0 the text

>*Jeani*

Then write into record 1 the text

>*YHELLO*

Get out of SUBTEST with Control-C. Make a copy of TESTFILE.TMP with the command

>*PIP SECOND.TMP=TESTFILE.TMP*

Rename the original file with the command

>*REN $$$.SUB=TESTFILE.TMP*

Then call the extended submit processor with the command

>*XSUB*

and verify that XSUB intercepts all console input requests, both those originating in CCP and those from the user program, YHELLO. Also verify that XSUB issues the message

>*(xsub active)*

Since no coldstart has been initiated, XSUB should still be active. Test whether it is by creating another $$$.SUB file with the command

REN $$$.SUB=SECOND.TMP

Verify that XSUB fails to respond to the question asked by YHELLO. Answer the question from the console. XSUB may appear to come back to life, but this time it isn't XSUB that has read the file $$$.SUB. When YHELLO jumped to 0000, a true warmboot was created. The presence of $$$.SUB caused CCP to shift into batch processing mode and read the file $$$.SUB. While active, XSUB searches the directory each time it intercepts a BDOS function 10. If $$$.SUB is not found, then XSUB restores the warmboot vector at location 0000 to point back into CBIOS. The next jump to 0000 will invoke a true warmboot. The true warmboot restores the vector at 0005 to point back to BDOS, and doing so puts XSUB out of business. The Digital Research manual is inaccurate on this point; coldboot is *not* required to disable XSUB.

Summary

If $$$.SUB exists at warmboot, CCP enters batch mode. In batch mode, CCP reads control statements from $$$.SUB instead of from the console. When $$$.SUB is exhausted, CCP exits batch mode. When XSUB is called, it loads itself just below CCP and sets the vectors at 0000 and 0005 to point into its own intercept processors. It then returns directly to CCP and waits for a BDOS function 10 to be called through the vector at 0005. The next BDOS function 10 will be filled from $$$.SUB, if this file exists. Otherwise, the vector at 0000 will be restored to point to CBIOS warmboot, and function 10 will be passed to BDOS for processing. This "half-active" state continues until the next time a program jumps to 0000. In this state, every function 10 causes XSUB to search for $$$.SUB and fill the console input request from $$$.SUB if this file is found. This state persists until a warmboot restores the vector at 0005 and thus fully disables XSUB.

CHAPTER 17

The USER Command

CP/M 2.2 *ASSIGNS* each file in the directory to a specific USER. The default is USER 0, and, normally, all existing files belong to USER 0. However, if you "go to control point 1," for example, by using the CCP command

> *USER 1*

and then create a file by, for example, the command

> *SAVE 6 TMP.COM*

then the new file TMP.COM will belong to USER 1 and will appear in the directory listing obtained by

> *DIR*

only while you are at control point 1. When you return to control point 0 with the CCP command

> *USER 0*

you will find that the file TMP.COM does not appear in the disk directory.

File Access via PIP

The CP/M 2.2 CCP command

> *USER x*

can be used to go to any of 16 control points numbered 0 through 15. While you are at control point 3, for example, you will have general access to, and only to, the files that belong to control point 3. The utility program PIP, however, can be used to copy files that belong to another control point. For example, while you are at control point 3, you can get a copy of STAT.COM from control point 0 by using the command

PIP STAT.COM=STAT.COM[G0]

But first you have to get a copy of PIP itself. To do so, you must first return to control point 0 by using the command

USER 0

Then load PIP.COM into memory with DDT by using the command

DDT PIP.COM

Get out of DDT with Control-C or G0, and then go back to control point 3 with the command

USER 3

Since the USER command is processed entirely by CCP, no code is loaded over the PIP.COM image still in memory. Save that image with the command

SAVE 30 PIP.COM

which will give you a copy of PIP on control point 3. With PIP you can now copy from control point 0 any other needed files and utility programs.

File Access via COMMON

To take better advantage of the control point facility under CP/M 2.2, however, what is needed is a simple way to gain read access to all the commonly used fixed utility programs such as PIP, ED, STAT, etc., without having to copy each one physically to each control point. Utility program COMMON, shown in Fig. 17.1, provides this access.

A file created by COMMON is called a *virtual file* because it has a directory entry but occupies no other disk space. Physically, a virtual file is a pointer into an existing real file. Any real file to which virtual files point should be treated as a nonerasable Read-Only file. Whenever any such "base" file is erased, all associated virtual files should be erased.

With COMMON installed in your system, the CCP command

COMMON STAT.COM

will create for the current user, for example USER 3, a virtual file providing read access to the file STAT.COM belonging to USER 0. USER 3 can then execute STAT. Similarly, to gain access to PIP, USER 3 could use the command

COMMON PIP.COM

```
                    ;File:  COMMON.ASM
                    ;Edit date:      81/01/08.
                    ;
                    ;          COMMON - Create a common file.
                    ;
                    ;
                    ;          CCP call:
                    ;
                    ;                    COMMON u:ufn
                    ;
                    ;          Create for the current user a Read-Only virtual
                    ;        ` file pointing into  ufn  of USER u.  The virtual
                    ;          file will occupy· a directory space but will use
                    ;          no other disk space.
                    ;
                    ;          Copyright 1981 by  microMethods
                    ;                            P.O. Box G
                    ;                            Warrenton, OR  97146
                    ;
                    ;
0005 =              BDOS     EQU     5
005C =              FCB      EQU     5CH
0080 =              SBUF     EQU     0080H
                    ;
                    ;          BDOS Functions.
                    ;
0009 =              MSGF     EQU     9
000F =              OPNF     EQU     15
0010 =              CLSF     EQU     16
0011 =              SFEF     EQU     17
0013 =              DELF     EQU     19
0016 =              MAKF     EQU     22
001E =       ·      SFAF     EQU     30
001F =              GDPB     EQU     31
0020 =              USRF     EQU     32
                    ;
0100                         ORG     100H
                    ;
0100 210000                  LXI     H,0000
0103 39                      DAD     SP
0104 225902                  SHLD    OLDSP
                    ;
0107 319D01                  LXI     SP,STACK
010A 0E09                    MVI     C,MSGF
010C 111901                  LXI     D,OLDU+1
010F CD0500                  CALL    BDOS
0112 C39D01                  JMP     COM
                    ;
0115 00             FLAG:    DB      0          ;Flag  0=file not found
0116                EXT:     DS      1          ;Logical ext's per phy ext
0117                USER:    DS      1
0118                OLDU:    DS      1
0119 436F707972              DB      'Copyright 1981 by microMethods.'
0138 24                      DB      '$'
0139                FNT:     DS      33+3
015D                         DS      2*32
019D                STACK:   DS      0
                    ;
019D 3A5C00         COM:     LDA     FCB        ;Check drop file
01A0 FEED                    CPI     '_'-'@'    and 0FFH
01A2 CAC502                  JZ      DRP        ;If drop file
                    ;
01A5 3A5C00                  LDA     FCB
01A8 321801                  STA     OLDU
                    ;
01AB 0E20                    MVI     C,USRF     ;Get current user #
01AD 1EFF                    MVI     E,0FFH
01AF CD0500                  CALL    BDOS
01B2 321701                  STA     USER
                    ;
                    ;          Get Extent Mask.
                    ;
01B5 0E1F                    MVI     C,GDPB
01B7 CD0500                  CALL    BDOS
01BA 110400                  LXI     D,4
01BD 19                      DAD     D
```

Fig. 17.1 Assembly listing of COMMON

```
01BE  7E              MOV    A,M
01BF  3C              INR    A
01C0  321601          STA    EXT      ;Log/phys = exm + 1
                  ;
01C3  0E20     COM1:  MVI    C,USRF   ;Set to user "B"
01C5  3A1801          LDA    OLDU
01C8  5F              MOV    E,A
01C9  CD0500          CALL   BDOS
                  ;
01CC  3E00            MVI    A,0      ;Clear auto select
01CE  325C00          STA    FCB
01D1  115C00          LXI    D,FCB    ;Find file
01D4  0E11            MVI    C,SFEF
01D6  CD0500          CALL   BDOS
01D9  FEFF            CPI    0FFH
01DB  CA4802          JZ     COM3     ;If done
                  ;
01DE  211501          LXI    H,FLAG   ;Mark file found
01E1  34              INR    M
                  ;
01E2  CDF602          CALL   FFA      ;Form directory entry address
01E5  115C00          LXI    D,FCB
01E8  0E20            MVI    C,32
01EA  CDED02          CALL   MMC
                  ;
01ED  0E20            MVI    C,USRF   ;Set back current user
01EF  3A1701          LDA    USER
01F2  5F              MOV    E,A
01F3  CD0500          CALL   BDOS
                  ;
01F6  215C00          LXI    H,FCB    ;Move FNT
01F9  113901          LXI    D,FNT
01FC  0E10            MVI    C,16
01FE  CDED02          CALL   MMC
                  ;
0201  113901          LXI    D,FNT    ;Create file
0204  0E16            MVI    C,MAKF
0206  CD0500          CALL   BDOS
0209  3C              INR    A
020A  CA5C02          JZ     COM5     ;If directory full
                  ;
020D  215C00          LXI    H,FCB    ;Move FNT + RBT
0210  113901          LXI    D,FNT
0213  0E20            MVI    C,32
0215  CDED02          CALL   MMC
                  ;
0218  3A6A00          LDA    FCB+0EH  ;Clear S2 high bit
021B  E67F            ANI    7FH
021D  326A00          STA    FCB+0EH
0220  0E10            MVI    C,CLSF   ;Close the file
0222  115C00          LXI    D,FCB
0225  CD0500          CALL   BDOS
                  ;
0228  3A6500          LDA    FCB+09   ;Mark it R/O
022B  F680            ORI    80H
022D  326500          STA    FCB+09
0230  0E1E            MVI    C,SFAF   ;SET R/O
0232  115C00          LXI    D,FCB
0235  CD0500          CALL   BDOS
                  ;
0238  216800          LXI    H,FCB+0CH       ;Advance extent
023B  3A1601          LDA    EXT
023E  86              ADD    M
023F  77              MOV    M,A
0240  E6E0            ANI    0E0H
0242  C26702          JNZ    COM7     ;If extent overflow
0245  C3C301          JMP    COM1
                  ;
0248  0E20     COM3:  MVI    C,USRF   ;Set back current user
024A  3A1701          LDA    USER
024D  5F              MOV    E,A
024E  CD0500          CALL   BDOS
0251  3A1501          LDA    FLAG     ;Check file found
```

Fig. 17.1 Assembly listing of COMMON (Cont.)

```
0254 B7                       ORA      A
0255 CA6D02                   JZ       COM8     ;If file not found
                     ;
0258 310000      COM4:        LXI      SP,0000
0259 =           OLDSP        EQU      $-2
025B C9                       RET
                     ;
                     ;        Process directory full error.
                     ;
025C 117302      COM5:        LXI      D,COMA   ;"No directory space"
025F 0E09        COM6:        MVI      C,MSGF
0261 CD0500                   CALL     BDOS
0264 C35802                   JMP      COM4
                     ;
                     ;        Process EXTent Overflow.
                     ;
0267 118802      COM7:        LXI      D,COMB   ;"Extent overflow"
026A C35F02                   JMP      COM6
                     ;
                     ;        Process file not found.
                     ;
026D 11B302      COM8:        LXI      D,COMC   ;"File not found"
0270 C35F02                   JMP      COM6
                     ;
0273 0D0A446972  COMA:        DB       0DH,0AH,'Directory is full.$'
0288 0D0A457874  COMB:        DB       0DH,0AH,'Extent overflow: File too big to COMMON.$'
02B3 0D0A46696C  COMC:        DB       0DH,0AH,'File not found.$'
                     ;
                     ;        Process Dropfile.
                     ;
02C5 3E00        DRP:         MVI      A,0      ;Open the file
02C7 325C00                   STA      FCB
02CA 115C00                   LXI      D,FCB
02CD 0E0F                     MVI      C,OPNF
02CF CD0500                   CALL     BDOS
                     ;
02D2 3A6500                   LDA      FCB+09   ;Clear R/O
02D5 E67F                     ANI      7FH
02D7 326500                   STA      FCB+09
02DA 0E1E                     MVI      C,SFAF
02DC 115C00                   LXI      D,FCB
02DF CD0500                   CALL     BDOS
                     ;
02E2 0E13                     MVI      C,DELF   ;Drop file
02E4 115C00                   LXI      D,FCB
02E7 CD0500                   CALL     BDOS
                     ;
02EA C35802                   JMP      COM4
                     ;
                     ;        MMC - Move (C) Bytes.
                     ;        Entry   HL = Source fwa
                     ;                DE = Destination fwa
                     ;                C = byte count
                     ;
02ED 7E          MMC:         MOV      A,M
02EE 12                       STAX     D
02EF 13                       INX      D
02F0 23                       INX      H
02F1 0D                       DCR      C
02F2 C2ED02                   JNZ      MMC      ;Loop for (C) bytes
02F5 C9                       RET
                     ;
                     ;        FFA - Form File Address.
                     ;        Entry    A = FNT ordinal
                     ;        Exit     HL = FNT address
                     ;
02F6 B7          FFA:         ORA      A
02F7 1717171717               RAL ! RAL ! RAL ! RAL ! RAL     ;*32
02FC 5F                       MOV      E,A
02FD 1600                     MVI      D,0
02FF 218000                   LXI      H,SBUF
0302 19                       DAD      D
0303 C9                       RET
```

Fig. 17.1 *Assembly listing of COMMON (Cont.)*

Directory space is the only system resource consumed by the virtual file created by COMMON.

Calling COMMON

The general CCP command format is

COMMON u:ufn

where u designates the source USER and ufn is an unambiguous filename. COMMON will go to the control point of USER u, search there for the file named ufn, and if this is found, create for the calling user a read-only file pointing into the named file.

The USER designator u is blank for USER 0 but is one of the character set [A, B, C, D, E, F, G, H, I, J, K, L, M, N, O] corresponding to USER [1, 2, 3, 4, 5, 6, 7, 8, 9, 10, 11, 12, 13, 14, 15].

Deleting a COMMON File

A read-only file cannot, of course, be erased, but you can delete a virtual file by using the command

COMMON — :ufn

The minus sign (−) employed as USER designator causes COMMON to delete the directory entry for the file ufn, thus making it unavailable to the current user.

Whenever any doubt exists as to whether the base file has been erased or updated, simply delete your virtual file and re-access the base file with

COMMON — :ufn
COMMON u:ufn

Since only one user can be active at any given time on a CP/M system, this facility provides simple multi-user access to a dynamic data base. Even if you have a large number of data-base files to be accessed, it would be practical to provide each user with a SUBMIT file containing the requisite virtual file delete and access commands and to process the SUBMIT file as a part of the user log-in procedure.

A Virtual COMMON

Normally, you will use DDT to get COMMON itself to your control point. An example sequence might be

USER 0
DDT COMMON.COM
G0

> *USER 3*
> *SAVE 2 COMMON.COM*

This sequence creates a real copy of COMMON.COM on control point 3.

If we really want to conserve disk space, we can now use our real COMMON to create a virtual COMMON. Then we can erase the real one. The continued sequence for doing so might be

> *REN TMP.COM=COMMON.COM*
> *TMP COMMON.COM*
> *ERA TMP.COM*

This sequence releases the disk space occupied by our real copy of COMMON but leaves us still owning an executable virtual COMMON. Our virtual COMMON, of course, has all of the same capabilities as the real COMMON.

Summary

The USER facility provides a way to partition available disk space effectively. When several users or applications share the computer system, these partitions can help protect against accidental file modification or erasure. Commonly needed read-only files can be efficiently accessed across all partitions through the COMMON utility program.

CHAPTER 18

Recovering an Erased File

A *CP/M FILE* is erased by entering the hex value E5 into byte 00 of each extent of the file appearing in the disk directory and by releasing in the RBR all record blocks reserved for the file. The file itself, and, indeed, each of its directory entries, or physical extents, remains intact until such time as a subsequent disk operation overwrites either a directory entry or a record block formerly reserved for the file. Until such time as a subsequent write operation occurs on the disk, an erased file can be retrieved by setting back to 00 the first byte of each of its directory entries. A warmstart, for example, can then be performed to restore the reservation of the record blocks in the RBR.

Recall that in Chap. 6 we wrote a program named DIRSIZE that used the CP/M search for file functions 17 and 18 (called *search for first occurrence* and *search for next occurrence*) to count all of the occupied directory entry spaces in the disk directory. If we put a question mark (?) into byte 00 of the file control block referenced by the search function, CP/M will return any matched entry, "allocated or free." It is the "or free" that is of interest to our present purpose. A "free" entry in the disk directory is an erased directory entry.

In this chapter we will present a CP/M 2.2 utility program designed not only to recover erased files but to address complications that can arise—complications that we will discuss in some detail.

Restore

When given a file name, such as TEST.TMP, in a command such as

RESTORE TEST.TMP

the program named RESTORE, shown in Fig. 18.1, uses BDOS functions 17 and 18 to search the entire directory for all occurrences of the file name TEST.TMP, allocated or free, that is, active or erased. If an active entry is found for this name, then RESTORE will issue the message:

File not erased

```
                    ;File:   RESTORE.ASM
                    ;
                    ;       Restore an ERAsed file.
                    ;
                    ;       CP/M call:    RESTORE ufn
                    ;
                    ;       Assembly constants.
                    ;
      0005 =        BDOS    EQU     0005H
      005C =        SFCB    EQU     005CH
      0080 =        SBUFF   EQU     0080H
                    ;
                    ;       BDOS functions.
                    ;
      0009 =        MSGF    EQU     9          ;Write console message
      000A =        RDCF    EQU     10         ;Read console line
      000C =        VERF    EQU     12         ;Read CP/M version
      000E =        SELF    EQU     14         ;Select disk
      0010 =        CLOF    EQU     16         ;Close file
      0011 =        SFEF    EQU     17         ;Find first occurence
      0012 =        SFNF    EQU     18         ;Find next occurence
      0016 =        MAKF    EQU     22         ;Create file
      001A =        DMAF    EQU     26         ;Set DMA
      001F =        DPBF    EQU     31         ;Get DPB fwa
      0025 =        RSDF    EQU     37         ;Reset (log-out) disk drive
                    ;
      0100          ORG     0100H
                    ;
      0100 31AF01   LXI     SP,STACK
      0103 C3AF01   JMP     REF
                    ;
                    ;       Data space.
                    ;
      0106 00       DBNDX:  DB      0          ;Directory-entry buffer index
      0107 00       DBTMP:  DB      0          ;Temp for count
      0108 00       CHTMP:  DB      0          ;Temp for 2nd char
                    ;
      0109 3F       FCB:    DB      '?'
      010A 0000000000  DB   0,0,0,0,0,0,0,0
      0112 000000         DB   0,0,0
      0115 00000000  EXT:  DB   0,0,0,0
      0119 0000000000  DB   0,0,0,0,0,0,0,0,0,0,0,0,0,0,0,0
      0129 00000000  NR:   DB   0,0,0,0
                    ;
      012D 40       CBUFF:  DB      64         ;Console input buffer
      012E          DS      64+1
                    ;
      016F          DS      2*32
      01AF =        STACK   EQU     $
                    ;
      01AF 215D00   REF:    LXI     H,SFCB+1   ;Get the filename
      01B2 110A01   LXI     D,FCB+1
      01B5 0E0B     MVI     C,11
      01B7 CD1F04   CALL    MMC
                    ;
      01BA 3A5C00   LDA     SFCB       ;Select disk
      01BD B7       ORA     A
      01BE CAC801   JZ      REF1       ;If no selection
                    ;
      01C1 3D       DCR     A
      01C2 5F       MOV     E,A
      01C3 0E0E     MVI     C,SELF
      01C5 CD0500   CALL    BDOS
```

Fig. 18.1 *Assembly listing of RESTORE*

```
                  ;
01C8 3E00    REF1:   MVI    A,0                  ;Reset directory-entry buffer
01CA 320601          STA    DBNDX
01CD 0E0C            MVI    C,VERF               ;Check CP/M 2.2
01CF CD0500          CALL   BDOS
01D2 7D              MOV    A,L
01D3 B7              ORA    A
01D4 CA7C02          JZ     REF9                 ;If not 2.x
                  ;
01D7 0E1F            MVI    C,DPBF               ;Get extent mask
01D9 CD0500          CALL   BDOS
01DC 110400          LXI    D,4
01DF 19              DAD    D
01E0 7E              MOV    A,M
01E1 2F              CMA
01E2 320203          STA    MFNA
                  ;
01E5 118000          LXI    D,SBUFF              ;Set DMA
01E8 0E1A            MVI    C,DMAF
01EA CD0500          CALL   BDOS
                  ;
01ED 0E11            MVI    C,SFEF   ;Find first occurence
01EF 110901          LXI    D,FCB
01F2 CD0500          CALL   BDOS
01F5 FEFF            CPI    0FFH
01F7 CA4502          JZ     REF5                 ;If file not found
                  ;
01FA CD0704    REF2:   CALL   FFA                  ;Set HL=FNT address
01FD E5              PUSH   H
01FE 110A01          LXI    D,FCB+1
0201 23              INX    H
0202 0E0B            MVI    C,11
0204 CD1504          CALL   KST                  ;Compare strings
0207 D1              POP    D
0208 C22202          JNZ    REF3                 ;If not our filename
                  ;
                  ;  We have a directory entry with matching filename.
                  ;
020B 210601          LXI    H,DBNDX              ;Get buffer index
020E 7E              MOV    A,M
020F 34              INR    M                    ;Advance buffer index
0210 6F              MOV    L,A                  ;Set HL=next buffer loc
0211 2600            MVI    H,0
0213 2929292929      DAD H ! DAD H ! DAD H ! DAD H ! DAD H   ;*32
0218 013004          LXI    B,MBUFF
021B 09              DAD    B
                  ;
021C EB              XCHG                        ;Save the directory entry
021D 0E20            MVI    C,32
021F CD1F04          CALL   MMC
                  ;
                  ;  Search for next occurence.
                  ;
0222 0E12    REF3:   MVI    C,SFNF
0224 CD0500          CALL   BDOS
0227 FEFF            CPI    0FFH
0229 C2FA01          JNZ    REF2                 ;Loop to end of directory
                  ;
                  ;  We have searched the entire directory.
                  ;
022C 3A0601          LDA    DBNDX                ;Check file found
022F B7              ORA    A
0230 CA4502          JZ     REF5                 ;If file not found
                  ;
                  ;  If file not erased, then don't restore it.
                  ;
0233 CDF303          CALL   CFE                  ;Check file erased
0236 C25002          JNZ    REF7                 ;If file not erased
                  ;
                  ;  If multiple erased files, issue a warning.
                  ;
0239 CDBD03          CALL   CME                  ;Check multiple entries
023C C25602          JNZ    REF8                 ;If more than one file
                  ;
                  ;  Restore the file.
                  ;
023F CD1C03          CALL   RAE                  ;Restore all extents
```

Fig. 18.1 *Assembly listing of RESTORE (Cont.)*

```
0242 C30000    REF4:   JMP     0000            ;Warmboot
               ;
               ;       File not found.
               ;
0245 118202    REF5:   LXI     D,REFA          ;"File not found."
0248 0E09      REF6:   MVI     C,MSGF
024A CD0500            CALL    BDOS
024D C34202            JMP     REF4
               ;
               ;       File not erased.
               ;
0250 119202    REF7:   LXI     D,REFB          ;"File not erased."
0253 C34802            JMP     REF6
               ;
               ;       Multiple identical extent numbers found.
               ;
0256 11A302    REF8:   LXI     D,REFC          ;"Multiple files found."
0259 0E09              MVI     C,MSGF
025B CD0500            CALL    BDOS
025E 0E0A              MVI     C,RDCF          ;Read response
0260 112D01            LXI     D,CBUFF
0263 CD0500            CALL    BDOS
0266 3A2F01            LDA     CBUFF+2
0269 E65F              ANI     5FH
026B FE59              CPI     'Y'
026D C24202            JNZ     REF4            ;If not "yes"
               ;
               ;       Close each extent under a unique name.
               ;
0270 CDEA02            CALL    MFN             ;Modify all file names
0273 CD1C03            CALL    RAE             ;Restore all
0276 CD6103            CALL    DFN             ;Display new filenames
0279 C34202            JMP     REF4
               ;
               ;       We need CP/M 2.x.
               ;
027C 11CE02    REF9:   LXI     D,REFD          ;"Need 2.x"
027F C34802            JMP     REF6
               ;
0282 46696C6520 REFA:  DB      'File not found.$'
0292 46696C6520 REFB:  DB      'File not erased.$'
02A3 4D756C7469 REFC:  DB      'Multiple files found.'
02B8 0D0A526573 REFD:  DB      0DH,0AH,'Restore all? (Y/N):$'
02CE 5468697320 REFD:  DB      'This program needs CP/M 2.x$'
               ;
               ;       MFN - Modify all Filenames.
               ;       Insert unique 2nd character into each filename.
               ;       Set 3rd filename char to "A" for phy ext 0, "B" for 1,
               ;       Mark all extents 00.
               ;
02EA 3A0601    MFN:    LDA     DBNDX
02ED 320701            STA     DBTMP
02F0 213204            LXI     H,MBUFF+2       ;2nd char
02F3 113C04            LXI     D,MBUFF+0CH     ;ext
02F6 012000            LXI     B,32
02F9 3E41              MVI     A,'A'
               ;
02FB 77        MFN1:   MOV     M,A             ;Insert new 2nd char
02FC 3C                INR     A
02FD 320801            STA     CHTMP
0300 1A                LDAX    D               ;Set 3rd char = "ext"
0301 E6FF              ANI     0FFH            ;Extent mask
0302 =         MFNA    EQU     $-1
0303 C641              ADI     'A'
0305 23                INX     H
0306 77                MOV     M,A
0307 2B                DCX     H
0308 AF                XRA     A               ;Set ext = 00
0309 12                STAX    D
               ;
030A EB                XCHG
030B 09                DAD     B
030C EB                XCHG
030D 09                DAD     B
               ;
030E 3A0701            LDA     DBTMP
0311 3D                DCR     A
```

Fig. 18.1 *Assembly listing of RESTORE (Cont.)*

```
0312 320701              STA     DBTMP
0315 3A0801              LDA     CHTMP
0318 C2FB02              JNZ     MFN1        ;Loop over all extents
031B C9                 RET
            ;
            ;
            ;            RAE - Restore All Extents.
            ;
031C 3E00    RAE:        MVI     A,0
031E 320901              STA     FCB
0321 3A0601              LDA     DBNDX
0324 4F                 MOV     C,A
0325 213104              LXI     H,MBUFF+1
            ;
0328 C5      RAE1:       PUSH    B
0329 0E0F                MVI     C,15
032B 110A01              LXI     D,FCB+1
032E CD1F04              CALL    MMC         ;Move filename
0331 E5                 PUSH    H
0332 110901              LXI     D,FCB
0335 0E16                MVI     C,MAKF      ;Create directory entry
0337 CD0500              CALL    BDOS
033A 3A1701              LDA     FCB+0EH     ;Clear "not-written" bit
033D E67F                ANI     7FH
033F 321701              STA     FCB+0EH
0342 E1                 POP     H           ;Points to RBT image
0343 2B                 DCX     H           ;Get record count
0344 7E                 MOV     A,M
0345 111801              LXI     D,FCB+15
0348 12                 STAX    D
0349 13                 INX     D
034A 23                 INX     H
034B 0E10                MVI     C,16
034D CD1F04              CALL    MMC
0350 E5                 PUSH    H
0351 110901              LXI     D,FCB       ;Close current extent
0354 0E10                MVI     C,CLOF
0356 CD0500              CALL    BDOS
0359 E1                 POP     H
035A C1                 POP     B
035B 23                 INX     H
035C 0D                 DCR     C
035D C22803              JNZ     RAE1        ;Loop over all extents
0360 C9                 RET
            ;
            ;            DFN - Display New Filenames.
            ;
0361 119603  DFN:        LXI     D,DFNA      ;"File names created:"
0364 0E09                MVI     C,MSGF
0366 CD0500              CALL    BDOS
0369 3A0601              LDA     DBNDX
036C 213104              LXI     H,MBUFF+1
            ;
036F E5      DFN1:       PUSH    H
0370 320701              STA     DBTMP
0373 11AE03              LXI     D,DFNB      ;Move file name
0376 0E08                MVI     C,8
0378 CD1F04              CALL    MMC
037B 13                 INX     D           ;Move file type
037C 0E03                MVI     C,3
037E CD1F04              CALL    MMC
0381 11AE03              LXI     D,DFNB
0384 0E09                MVI     C,MSGF
0386 CD0500              CALL    BDOS
0389 E1                 POP     H
038A 012000              LXI     B,32
038D 09                 DAD     B
038E 3A0701              LDA     DBTMP
0391 3D                 DCR     A
0392 C26F03              JNZ     DFN1        ;Loop for all extents
0395 C9                 RET
            ;
0396 0D0A46696CDFNA:     DB      0DH,0AH,'File names created:',0DH,0AH,'$'
03AE 2020202020DFNB:     DB      '        .   ',0DH,0AH,'$'
            ;
            ;            CME - Check Multiple Erased Entries.
            ;            Exit   Z = true, if one file found
```

Fig. 18.1 *Assembly listing of RESTORE (Cont.)*

```
                    ;                       E = file count
                    ;
03BD 3A0601   CME:    LDA     DBNDX
03C0 4F               MOV     C,A
03C1 213C04           LXI     H,MBUFF+0CH      ;Point to ext bytes
                    ;
03C4 7E       CME1:   MOV     A,M
03C5 CDD203           CALL    CIE              ;Count identical extents
03C8 C0               RNZ                      ;If multiple files found
                    ;
03C9 112000           LXI     D,32
03CC 19               DAD     D
03CD 0D               DCR     C
03CE C2C403           JNZ     CME1             ;Loop over all extents
03D1 C9               RET
                    ;
                    ;   CIE - Count Identical Extents.
                    ;   Entry   A = current extent
                    ;   Exit    Z = true, if one such extent found
                    ;           E = extent count
                    ;
03D2 E5C5     CIE:    PUSH H ! PUSH B
03D4 1E00             MVI     E,0
03D6 210601           LXI     H,DBNDX
03D9 4E               MOV     C,M
03DA 213C04           LXI     H,MBUFF+0CH
                    ;
03DD 46       CIE1:   MOV     B,M
03DE B8               CMP     B
03DF C2E303           JNZ     CIE2             ;If not same extent
03E2 1C               INR     E                ;Advance extent count
03E3 D5       CIE2:   PUSH    D
03E4 112000           LXI     D,32
03E7 19               DAD     D
03E8 D1               POP     D
03E9 0D               DCR     C
03EA C2DD03           JNZ     CIE1             ;Loop over all extents
                    ;
03ED 7B               MOV     A,E              ;Check extents found
03EE FE01             CPI     1
03F0 C1E1             POP B ! POP H
03F2 C9               RET
                    ;
                    ;   CFE - Check file erased.
                    ;   Exit    Z = true, if file erased
                    ;
03F3 3A0601   CFE:    LDA     DBNDX
03F6 4F               MOV     C,A
03F7 213004           LXI     H,MBUFF
03FA 112000           LXI     D,32
                    ;
03FD 7E       CFE1:   MOV     A,M
03FE FEE5             CPI     0E5H
0400 C0               RNZ                      ;If unerased extent found
                    ;
0401 19               DAD     D
0402 0D               DCR     C
0403 C2FD03           JNZ     CFE1             ;Loop over all extents
0406 C9               RET
                    ;
                    ;   FFA - Form File Address.
                    ;   Entry   A = FNT ordinal
                    ;   Exit    HL = FNT address
                    ;
0407 B7       FFA:    ORA     A
0408 1717171717       RAL ! RAL ! RAL ! RAL ! RAL    ;*32
040D 5F               MOV     E,A
040E 1600             MVI     D,0
0410 218000           LXI     H,SBUFF
0413 19               DAD     D
0414 C9               RET
                    ;
                    ;   KST - Compare strings.
                    ;   Entry   HL = string1 fwa
                    ;           DE = strint2 fwa
                    ;            C = string compare length
```

Fig. 18.1 *Assembly listing of RESTORE (Cont.)*

```
                      ;      Exit     Z = true, if string1 = string2
                      ;
    0415 1A    KST:   LDAX    D
    0416 BE           CMP     M
    0417 C0           RNZ                   ;If mismatch
                      ;
    0418 23           INX     H
    0419 13           INX     D
    041A 0D           DCR     C
    041B C21504       JNZ     KST           ;Loop over compare length
    041E C9           RET
                      ;
                      ;      MMC - Move Memory.
                      ;      Entry   HL = source fwa
                      ;              DE = destination fwa
                      ;               C = byte count
                      ;
    041F 7E    MMC:   MOV     A,M
    0420 12           STAX    D
    0421 23           INX     H
    0422 13           INX     D
    0423 0D           DCR     C
    0424 C21F04       JNZ     MMC     ;Loop for C bytes
    0427 C9           RET
                      ;
    0430              ORG     16*($/16)+16
                      ;
    0430 =     MBUFF  EQU     $
```

Fig. 18.1 *Assembly listing of RESTORE (Cont.)*

and return control to CCP. Otherwise, the program will restore all erased extents of the named file. If no writing has occurred on the disk since TEST.TMP was erased, restoration of all its directory entries probably will recover the file intact.

Multiple Files

The first complication arises from the possibility of multiple erased files of the same name. To see how this situation might occur, consider the following command sequence:

> SAVE 1 FILE1.TMP
> SAVE 1 FILE2.TMP
> ERA FILE2.TMP
> REN FILE2.TMP=FILE1.TMP
> ERA FILE2.TMP

This sequence creates two erased directory entries, the FNT half of each entry containing the name FILE2.TMP. No information exists in the directory on which of these two entries was the last erased. In other words, there is no way to decide which entry to restore. Under CP/M 2.2, the two files in this simple example happen to contain the same information, and therefore it doesn't matter which one we restore. But in general, when more than one directory entry is found, an examination of file contents is the only way to determine which directory entry represents the file of interest.

Multiple Extents

Larger files can cause additional complications. Consider, for example, the directory residue of the following command sequence:

> *SAVE 200 FILE3.TMP*
> *SAVE 200 FILE4.TMP*
>
> *ERA FILE4.TMP*
> *REN FILE4.TMP=FILE3.TMP*
> *ERA FILE4.TMP*

The disk space required to hold 200 pages of 256 bytes each is 50k bytes, or just over three CP/M logical extents of 16k each. On any disk arranged with less than four logical extents per directory entry, each of these files will have two or more directory entries, or physical extents. On a single-density disk, this example command sequence will create eight erased directory entries all containing the file name FILE4.TMP. There will be two extents number 00, two extents number 01, two extents number 02, and two extents number 03. To determine which one of each extent pair is the actual representative of the file of interest, an examination of file content is necessary.

Whenever RESTORE finds identical extents, it makes no attempt to resolve complications. Instead, it simply restores all extents and gives each a unique file name. When RESTORE finds, for example, the two small files named FILE2.TMP, it will restore each of the files and give them the names FAAE2.TMP and FBA2.TMP. The unique file name is created by changing second and third characters of each directory entry. The second character is made unique for each entry simply by assigning A to the first directory entry found, B to the second, C to the third, and so on.

The third character of the unique name reveals the original physical extent. Suppose, for example, that your system has two logical extents per physical extent and that the file named FXX.TMP is a large file with two physical extents, that is, two directory entries. Suppose that we erase this file and then restore it with the command

> *RESTORE FXX.TMP*

If no duplicate extents are found, the file will be immediately restored. If RESTORE finds any duplicate extents, it will issue the message

> *Multiple files found.*
> *Restore all? (Y/N):*

and wait for your response. Any answer other than Y will cause RESTORE to return directly to CCP with no file restoration attempted. If you answer Y, RESTORE will restore each discovered extent under a unique name and as a "zeroth" extent. For example, existence of two physical extents 0 and two physical extents 1 could yield the files

> *FAA.TMP*
> *FBC.TMP*
> *FCA.TMP*
> *FDC.TMP*

The second character of the file name simply shows the order in which the entries were encountered in the directory. Equally possible sets of file names would be

FBA.TMP
FAA.TMP
FCC.TMP
FDC.TMP

or

FCA.TMP
FDA.TMP
FBC.TMP
FAC.TMP

All first extents have A for their third character, and all second extents have C for their third character. When, as in this example, there are two logical extents per physical extent, the letter B will never appear as an extent indicator because it is deleted by applying what is known as the *extent mask*. If we didn't delete it, a first extent might be marked either A or B in the third character of the restored file name, and things would be even more confusing.

Summary

Complications encountered when we attempt file restoration arise from a formidable source. The CP/M file erase operation, although apparently trivial, is fundamentally irreversible.

If you have not written on the disk since the file was erased, there is a good chance the file can be restored. In the event that multiple-directory entries confound the recovery process, RESTORE gives you the ability to examine each extent individually and thereby derive information that is possibly sufficient to piece the file back together.

ASCII Character Code Table

00 NUL	20 SP	40 @	60 `
01 SOH	21 !	41 A	61 a
02 STX	22 "	42 B	62 b
03 ETX	23 #	43 C	63 c
04 EOT	24 $	44 D	64 d
05 ENQ	25 %	45 E	65 e
06 ACK	26 &	46 F	66 f
07 BEL	27 '	47 G	67 g
08 BS	28 (	48 H	68 h
09 HT	29)	49 I	69 i
0A LF	2A *	4A J	6A j
0B VT	2B +	4B K	6B k
0C FF	2C ,	4C L	6C l
0D CR	2D –	4D M	6D m
0E SO	2E .	4E N	6E n
0F SI	2F /	4F O	6F o
10 DLE	30 0	50 P	70 p
11 DC1 (X-ON)	31 1	51 Q	71 q
12 DC2 (TAPE)	32 2	52 R	72 r
13 DC3 (X-OFF)	33 3	53 S	73 s
14 DC4	34 4	54 T	74 t
15 NAK	35 5	55 U	75 u
16 SYN	36 6	56 V	76 v
17 ETB	37 7	57 W	77 w
18 CAN	38 8	58 X	78 x
19 EM	39 9	59 Y	79 y
1A SUB	3A :	5A Z	7A z
1B ESC	3B ;	5B [	7B {
1C FS	3C <	5C \	7C ¦
1D GS	3D =	5D]	7D } (Alt mode)
1E RS	3E >	5E ^	7E ~
1F US	3F ?	5F _	7F DEL (Rubout)

CP/M 2.2 BDOS Functions Table

FNC	HEX	FUNCTION NAME	INPUTS	OUTPUTS
0	00	System Reset	none	none
1	01	Console Input	none	A=char
2	02	Console Output	E=char	none
3	03	Reader Input	none	A=char
4	04	Punch Output	E=char	none
5	05	List Output	E=char	none
6	06	Direct Console I/O	see def	see def
7	07	Get I/O Byte	none	A=(0003)
8	08	Set I/O Byte	E=iobyte	none
9	09	Print string$	DE=.string	none
10	0A	Read Console Buffer	DE=.buffer	string
11	0B	Get Console Status	none	A=status
12	0C	Get Version Number	none	HL=version
13	0D	Reset Disk System	none	see def
14	0E	Select Disk	E=disk	see def
15	0F	Open File	DE=.fcb	A=dir code
16	10	Close File	DE=.fcb	A=dir code
17	11	Search for first occurence	DE=.fcb	A=dir code
18	12	Search for next occurence	none	A=dir code
19	13	Delete File	DE=.fcb	A=dir code
20	14	Read Sequential	DE=.fcb	A=error code
21	15	Write Sequential	DE=.fcb	A=error code
22	16	Create New File	DE=.fcb	A=dir code
23	17	Rename File	DE=.fcb	A=dir code
24	18	Return Login Vector	none	HL=login vector
25	19	Return Current Disk	none	A=disk number
26	1A	Set DMA Address	DE=dma	none
27	1B	Get RBR Address	none	HL=.RBR
28	1C	Write Protect Disk	none	see def
29	1D	Get R/O Vector	none	HL=R/O vector
30	1E	Set File Attributes	DE=.fcb	see def
31	1F	Get DPB Address	none	HL=.DPB
32	20	Set or Get USER Code	see def	see def
33	21	Read Random	DE=.fcb	A=error code
34	22	Write Random	DE=.fcb	A=error code
35	23	Compute File Size	DE=.fcb	r0, r1, ov set
36	24	Set Random Record	DE=.fcb	r0, r1, ov set
37	25	Reset Drive	DE=drive vector	A=00
38	26	No operation		
39	27	No operation		
40	28	Write Random with Zero Fill	DE=.fcb	A=error code

see def = see definition in Digital Research manual "CP/M 2.2
Interface Guide."

APPENDIX **C**

CBIOS Details

If your computer is an Intel MDS-800, then Digital Research may have provided your CBIOS; otherwise, your system integrator will have provided it. CBIOS is responsible for all physical transfer of information between peripheral devices and CP/M. CP/M 2.2 is designed to handle up to four character-oriented devices—a console, a printer, a punch, and a reader—and up to sixteen disk drives. A typical CP/M system includes the console and printer and two or more disk drives. One of the disk drives should be a floppy-disk drive capable of single-density operation. The 8-inch single-density disk is the medium used by Digital Research, and many others, for the distribution of CP/M software.

CBIOS is a set of customized basic input and output subroutines. As illustrated in Fig. C.1, it is the hardware interface of CP/M. CCP, and all standard CP/M user programs, communicate only with BDOS. CCP never communicates directly with CBIOS, and BDOS never communicates directly with any device. All peripheral operations, including disk operations, are provided solely by CBIOS. This partitioning of functions into "logical" operations in BDOS and "physical" operations in CBIOS is responsible for an important internal attribute of the structure of CP/M: CCP and BDOS are invariant across all systems running under CP/M 2.2. All hardware differences between systems are taken care of entirely in CBIOS.

In this section we will discuss the CBIOS entry points defined by Digital Research for CP/M 2.2. For certain utility programs, direct calls to CBIOS will always be necessary. SYSGEN, for example, must call CBIOS directly in order to read or write disk system tracks.

With respect to CP/M 2.2, although there is but one BDOS, there can be as

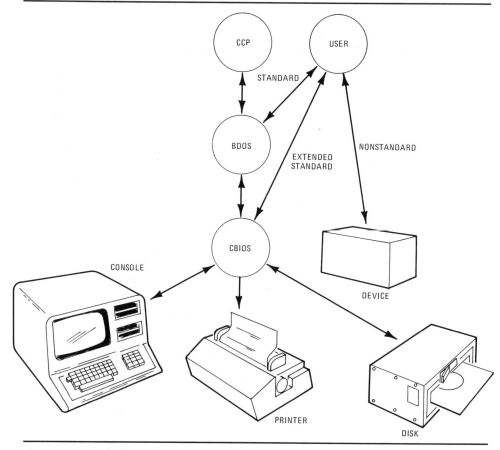

Fig. C.1 *CCP and all standard CP/M user programs communicate only with BDOS; BDOS communicates with peripheral devices (including disk devices) only through CBIOS*

many versions of CBIOS as there are system integrators to write them. Every CBIOS must begin with a specified list of 17 jump instructions that provide standardized entry into the 17 primary subroutines of which CBIOS is composed.

Two entry points process system start and restart. Seven entry points process characters to and from the console, printer, punch, and reader. The remaining eight entry points process operations related to sending CP/M sectors to the disk and receiving CP/M sectors from the disk.

A CBIOS always begins with these 17 jump instructions:

JMP BOOT	Complete a coldboot
JMP WBOOT	Process warmboot
JMP CONST	Console status
JMP CONIN	Console input
JMP CONOUT	Console output
JMP LIST	Printer output
JMP PUNCH	Punch output

JMP READER	Reader input
JMP HOME	Set track zero
JMP SELDSK	Select disk
JMP SETTRK	Set track
JMP SETSEC	Set sector
JMP SETDMA	Set DMA
JMP READ	Read CP/M sector
JMP WRITE	Write CP/M sector
JMP LISTST	Printer status
JMP SECTRAN	Skew CP/M sector

The discussion of these entry points in this section supplements the discussion of CBIOS in the Digital Research manual, "CP/M 2.2 Alteration Guide." Here we will restate the specification for each CBIOS entry point and provide additional commentary.

Your own CBIOS may contain more than 17 entry points. Additional entry points, and their purpose and function, should be documented by your system integrator. Transportable CP/M programs must limit their direct CBIOS calls to the 17 entry points defined by Digital Research. CP/M programs that you may wish to use under MP/M should not make direct calls to CBIOS. Any CP/M program that makes "extended standard" direct calls to CBIOS will have limited transportability; the word "transportability," as used here, refers to usability.

A program designed to control the stepper motors and pen solenoid of a graphics plotter will communicate with the device through a direct "non-standard" arrangement, as shown in Fig. C.1. Even well designed nonstandard programs can be transported only between computers similarly equipped.

CP/M 2.2 CBIOS Entry Points

BOOT = CBIOS + 00H

For this entry point, issue any sign-on message, and set up the warmboot vector at 0000 and the BDOS vector at 0005. Then jump to CCP with the initial disk and USER numbers in the C-register. CCP sets the current USER number from the high four bits of the C-register and the current disk from the low four bits. The CBIOS code that issues the sign-on message frequently is located in buffer space subsequently overwritten by CP/M operation, and hence this entry point is usable only by the coldstart loader.

WBOOT = CBIOS + 03H

This is the CBIOS entry point to which linkage is provided by the vector at 0000. Control arrives here immediately after a user program terminates in a jump to 0000, as do many user programs such as PIP. The assumption in the specification of warmboot is that the user program may have overwritten CCP. The specification calls for warmboot to reload CCP and BDOS from disk. Some CBIOS implementations do reload both CCP and BDOS, but some reload only

CCP plus the first sector of BDOS. BDOS itself is seldom overwritten by a user program, but the serial number in the first six bytes of BDOS—essential to CCP operation—is within the transient program area and is equally likely as CCP to be overwritten.

Warmboot restores the warmboot vector at 0000 and the BDOS vector at 0005 and then jumps to CCP fwa with the current disk, obtained from location 0004 in the C-register. When entered at its first word address, CCP issues an initialize function (0D) to BDOS. This logs out all disks and then logs in the disk in drive A. CCP then selects and causes log-in of the disk given to it by the entry value of the C-register. The current USER is then set from the high-order four bits of C.

Exercise: Call DDT, set location 0004 to 51, and then warmboot with G0. You should come up at control point 5 on Drive B.

CONST = CBIOS + 06H
> Exit A = FF (true) if character ready
> = 00 (false) if no console input ready

This status permits CONIN delay to be avoided.

CONIN = CBIOS + 09H
> Exit A = ASCII character, high bit cleared

This routine reads a character from the console keyboard, waiting, if necessary, for a character to be typed.

CONOUT = CBIOS + 0CH
> Entry C = ASCII character

Wait until the console controller is ready to accept a character before transmitting the character given.

LIST = CBIOS + 0FH
> Entry C = ASCII character

Wait until the printer controller is ready to accept a character and then transmit the character given. Delay created by waiting for the controller to get ready can be avoided by testing the printer status via the LISTST entry point.

PUNCH = CBIOS + 12H
READER = CBIOS + 15H
Send a character to a punch device from C, or read a character into A from a reader device. These largely unused CBIOS entry points could help sidestep the problems associated with cursor positioning on CRT, or video, type console terminals since there is a direct path through BDOS to these character I/O devices

LISTST = CBIOS + 2DH
> Exit A = FF (true), if ready for next character
> = 00 (false), if not

This status routine was unfortunately omitted in CP/M 1.4.

HOME = CBIOS + 18H
This entry point is the same as SETTRK with BC = 0000.

SELDSK = CBIOS + 1BH
> Entry C = drive number
> Exit HL = 0000 if drive is nonexistent, that is, no DPH table exists
> = DPH table fwa for drive (C).

For the next disk operation, select the drive given by the value in the C-register. Return the address of the Disk Parameter Header (DPH) table. Drives are numbered 0 through 15 for A through P, respectively.

SETTRK = CBIOS + 1EH
> Entry BC = track

For the next disk operation, select the track stated.

SETSEC = CBIOS + 21H
> Entry BC = translated CP/M sector number

For the next disk operation, select the translated CP/M sector stated. For a discussion of the translated CP/M sector, see the section titled "The Sector" in this Appendix.

SETDMA = CBIOS + 24H
> Entry BC = DMA address

Set the disk memory address for the next disk operation to the address given in the BC register. This address specifies the starting location in memory of 128 bytes containing the information either to be written to a CP/M sector or to receive 128 bytes of information from a CP/M sector.

READ = CBIOS + 27H
> Exit A = 0, if no errors
> = 1, if disk read error

Read the CP/M sector specified by SETSEC, SETTRK, and SELDSK into the buffer specified by SETDMA.

WRITE = CBIOS + 2AH
> Exit A = 0, if no errors
> = 1, if disk write error

Write the CP/M sector from the buffer specified by SETDMA to the disk specified by SELDSK at the location specified by SETTRK and SETSEC.

The IBM 3740 floppy-disk sector preamble provides for each sector on the disk to be marked "deleted data" or "nondeleted data." This IBM feature is not used by CP/M, and all sectors, where the option exists, should be marked "nondeleted."

SECTRAN = CBIOS + 30H

> Entry BC = CP/M sector number
> Exit HL = translated CP/M sector number

Note that CP/M sector numbers start at zero on each track. The skew table in CBIOS translates CP/M sector to translated CP/M sector. The main purpose for this CBIOS entry point is to provide compatibility with the CP/M 1.4 single-density disk format. This compatibility is of permanent importance for the distribution of CP/M software. For higher capacity disks, the routine will probably return HL = BC. For further discussion of sector skew, see the section titled "The Sector" in this Appendix.

CBIOS Disk Definition Tables

The correspondence between 16 possible logical drives—A, B, C, D, E, F, G, H, I, J, K, L, M, N, O, and P—and their defining Disk Parameter Blocks (DPB) is provided by the Disk Parameter Header (DPH) table in CBIOS. Each entry in the DPH occupies 16 bytes. The first entry is for Drive A, the second for Drive B, and so on. Each entry contains eight 16-bit words. Each word for which CBIOS is responsible is an address of something in CBIOS. The eight words of the DPH are arranged as follows:

XLT	Skew table address, or 0000 if no CP/M sector skew is used.
0000 0000 0000	Three words provided for BDOS to use for temporary storage.
DIRBUF	Directory buffer address
DPB	Disk parameter block address
CST	Directory checksum table address
RBR	Allocation table address

If CP/M sector skew is to be used, a skew table must be provided to map each CP/M sector into a translated CP/M sector. The translation is requested by BDOS, which calls the CBIOS SECTRAN subroutine just before calling the CBIOS SETSEC subroutine. Although the skew or physical ordering of sectors can be arbitrary, it is customary to build the skew table by first defining the first physical sector to be equal to the first logical sector and then filling in the table by adding a "skew factor" to each preceding entry. For example, the CP/M 1.4 skew table

1, 7, 13, 19, 25, 5, 11, 17, 23, 3, 9, 15, 21, 2,
8, 14, 20, 26, 6, 12, 18, 24, 4, 10, 16, 22

actually skips six sectors—which constitute the CP/M 1.4 skew factor—between each two entries everywhere except between sectors 21 and 2, where seven sectors are skipped.

The directory buffer that must be provided by a CP/M 2.2 CBIOS sidesteps a CP/M 1.4 problem discussed in Appendix E. BDOS uses the directory buffer in a manner that permits one directory buffer to be sufficient for all disks.

The directory checksum table provides space in CBIOS for BDOS to store an eight-bit checksum for each CP/M sector of the directory. CST=0000 disables checksumming.

The RBR table provides space to store one bit for each record block defined on the disk. BDOS sets the bit to 1 to indicate that the corresponding Block is reserved or in use.

For the purpose of specifying a disk for CP/M, the following eight parameters completely define a given logical disk device:

FSN	First sector number on each track
LSN	Last sector number on each track
SKF	Skew factor
RBS	Reservation block size in bytes
NBL	Number of reservation blocks on the disk
NDR	Number of directory entries
CDR	Number of checksummed directory entries
NST	Number of system tracks

These eight parameters can be used to construct in CBIOS a table called the *Disk Parameter Block* (DPB). A given DPB can be used to define as many physical devices as conform to the definition stated. In other words, more than one DPH can point to the same DPB.

A disk parameter block contains the following entries:

DW	*SPT*	;Sectors/track
DB	*BSH*	;Block shift
DB	*BLM*	;Block mask
DB	*EXM*	;Extent mask
DW	*DSM*	;Block capacity − 1 = max block number
DW	*DRM*	;Directory size
DW	*ALB*	;Up to 16 directory RBR bits
DW	*CKS*	;Checksum vector size
DW	*OFF*	;Offset = reserved tracks

The nine parameters in this table can be calculated or copied from the eight parameters at the beginning of this section, as follows:

$$SPT = LSN - FSN + 1$$
$$BSH = \text{Log, base 2, of RBS}/128$$
$$BLM = (2 \text{ to power BSH}) - 1$$
$$EXM = (\text{Phy ext size}/16k) - 1$$

where

Phy ext size = RBS times 8, if NBL greater than 255
Phy ext size = RBS times 16, if NBL less than 256

$$DSM = NBL - 1$$
$$DRM = NDR - 1$$

Number of Directory Blocks = (NDR*32)/RBS.

$$ALB = 1 \text{ bit for each directory block left adjusted with 0 fill}$$
$$CKS = (DRM + 1)/4$$
$$OFF = NST$$

The word ALB provides a string of bits that is copied by BDOS into the first word of the disk RBR table at log-in time to reserve the blocks dedicated to the directory. Since directory size is defined by DBP entries DRM, ALB, and CKS, you can easily change it, but the operational restrictions discussed in Appendix D apply. You must treat as read-only any disk written by a CBIOS with different directory size parameters.

The Sector

Since the term *sector* takes three different meanings under CP/M 2.2, additional qualifying terms become necessary. BDOS continues at all times to deal only with what is called a *CP/M sector*, which always contains 128 bytes. This CP/M sector is sometimes called a *logical sector*, or *logical record*. The skew table defines a one-to-one correspondence between logical sectors and something we might want to call a *physical sector*. If we call the skewed sector a physical sector, however, we will have some trouble because the size of the actual physical sectors on a high capacity disk is rarely going to be 128 bytes. Hence the terminology suggested is this: We will call a *CP/M sector* the 128 bytes that BDOS calls a *sector*. The skew table, if used, will map a CP/M sector to a *translated CP/M sector*. On a high capacity disk, the translated CP/M sector will usually occupy half, or a quarter, or an eighth of some actual physical sector. The physical sector is also sometimes called the *host sector*.

BDOS is only slightly involved in the conversion of a CP/M sector to a translated CP/M sector. BDOS calls the CBIOS SECTRAN subroutine just before calling the SETSEC subroutine. Except for that slight involvement, BDOS deals only with CP/M sectors. It is the responsibility of CBIOS to "block" and "deblock" CP/M sectors into and out of the actual host physical sectors of the disk. Except for providing compatibility with the standard CP/M single-density disk, BDOS might just as well have been left completely out of the sector skew process because when CP/M sectors are imbedded inside larger physical sectors, there is no advantage to skewing the CP/M sectors. Skew saves time when applied to physical sectors. On most higher capacity CP/M disk systems, the BDOS skew mechanism will be disabled; SECTRAN will return HL = BC. Skew, when used, will be provided at the physical sector level by your CBIOS and will be totally invisible to BDOS, as it should be, since it is a device-dependent consideration.

Efficient reading of CP/M sectors blocked in larger physical sectors presents no complications for CBIOS. All it has to do is remember the physical disk, track, and sector description of the current host sector and compare these values with corresponding values developed from the current CP/M sector requested. If it has the requested CP/M sector in the host buffer, then it can satisfy the request without actually reading anything from the disk.

Writing a CP/M sector, on the other hand, can present a complication. The simple thing would be to develop the physical disk, track, and sector containing the CP/M sector to be written, read that physical sector into the host buffer, copy the CP/M sector into place in the host buffer, and then write out the host sector. A more efficient scheme would omit prereading the host sector, if that is possible. For example, when the first CP/M sector is being written into a newly reserved record block, prereading is never required. BDOS informs CBIOS of this situation when it exists.

The Extent Mask

There now exists in CP/M three meanings for, or uses of, the word *extent*. The unqualified word refers to the contents of byte 0C of the directory entry. The term *logical extent* always refers to 128 CP/M sectors, or 16k bytes. The term *physical extent* always refers to a single directory entry.

The contents of byte 0C of the directory entry always point to a logical extent. If one directory entry can reserve and address 16k, then the physical extent and the logical extent are identical, and the *extent mask* is 00. If one directory entry can hold two logical extents, then the low bit of byte 0C of the directory entry points to the current logical extent—that is, it points to one of the two logical extents that can exist within the physical extent—and the extent mask is 01, or one bit. This mask extracts the logical extent pointer from byte 0C of the directory entry.

If one directory entry can hold four logical extents, then the low two bits of byte 0C of the directory entry point to the current logical extent—that is, they point to one of the four logical extents that can exist within each physical extent—and the extent mask is 03, or two bits.

In similar fashion, if one physical extent can hold eight logical extents, then the extent mask is 07, or three bits, and for 16 logical extents per physical extent, the extent mask is 0F, or four bits. This exhausts the arrangements possible under CP/M 2.2.

Each physical extent must hold one or more logical extents. This condition restricts the minimum size of the record block whenever the disk is divided into more than 255 blocks, and consequently reservation block words must be used rather than reservation block bytes. A single RBT entry can hold eight reservation block words. The minimum block size under this arrangement is therefore 2k, giving 16k per RBT or 16k per physical extent—the minimum permitted.

On a disk divided into fewer than 256 blocks, since each RBT entry can hold 16 reservation block bytes, the minimum block size is 1k, giving 16k per physical extent. This is the CP/M 1.4 arrangement.

The extent mask tells us how many logical extents there are in each physical extent. We can therefore tabulate the correlation between CP/M 2.2 extent masks and the ratio of logical to physical extents.

Logical ext/Physical ext	Extent mask
1	00
2	01
4	03
8	07
16	0F

The relation tabulated can be summarized by the formula

$$\text{Extent mask} = (\text{Physical ext size}/16k) - 1$$

where the physical extent size is eight times the block size if record block words are used and 16 times the block size if record block bytes are used. Record block bytes can be used to name record blocks only when the disk is divided into fewer than 256 blocks.

The extent mask for the current disk can be obtained from the disk parameter block in CBIOS, via BDOS function 31, using a sequence such as

```
MVI    C,31
CALL 0005
LXI    D,4
DAD    D
MOV   A,M      ;A = extent mask
INX    H
MOV   C,M      ;BC = number of Blocks − 1
INX    H
MOV   B,M
```

If the value in the B-register is nonzero, then record block words are being used.

Changing the CP/M 1.4 Directory Size

A standard CP/M 1.4 BDOS reserves two blocks for the directory. Each block can hold 32 directory entries. There are two bytes within BDOS that define the size of the directory. At relative location 003B past the first word address (fwa) of BDOS, you should find the hex value 3F, or 63 decimal. This is the maximum directory ordinal for the standard two-block directory. At relative location 003F past the fwa of BDOS, you should find the hex value C0, or 1100 0000 binary. The two bits that are set reserve block 00 and block 01 for the directory. At "initialize," this byte is stored into the first byte of the drive RBR. You can change the defined size of the directory by changing these two bytes.

For example, by reserving one more block for the directory, you can increase directory capacity from 64 to 96 entries. Here is one way to do this: Begin by calling SYSGEN to get an image of your CP/M system tracks into memory. When SYSGEN asks for a destination, give it a carriage return. This will cause SYSGEN to drop off and leave the system image in memory. Save this image with

SAVE 32 IMAGE.COM

Now load the image under DDT with the command

DDT IMAGE.COM

You should find BDOS beginning at location 1180 hex. At location 11BB = 1180 + 003B you should find the hex value 3F. This value equals the directory size minus 1. Change this to 5F, or 95 decimal. At location 11BF = 1180 + 003F you should find the value C0. Change this to E0, or 1110 0000 binary. This will reserve blocks 00, 01, and 02 for the directory.

Delete directory checksum processing by changing the byte at location 1577 = 1180 + 03F7 from 77 to 00 and by deleting the CALL instruction at location 158E = 1180 + 040E by changing CD xx B0 to 00 00 00.

Use G0, or Control-C, to get out of DDT. Call SYSGEN, and skip the "get" with a carriage return. Mount a disk to receive the new system, tell SYSGEN where it is, and then give SYSGEN a carriage return to cause the new system to be written.

A disk with a three-block directory, or other nonstandard size directory, should never be written upon by a CP/M system with standard directory parameters in its BDOS. Since there is nothing on the disk itself to indicate that the directory occupies more than two blocks, mixing systems may cause the extra directory blocks to be overwritten by a user file.

Moreover, a nonstandard BDOS should never be used to write on a disk already containing files written under a standard BDOS. A nonstandard BDOS will search the extra blocks for directory space. If it finds an entry space beginning with E5, it may write a directory entry there that may overwrite file information.

In other words, always treat as read-only any disk written under a BDOS different from the BDOS under which you are running.

Patching the CP/M 1.4 SAVE Command

There is a bug in the CP/M 1.4 SAVE command. When the file is closed by CCP, the DMA address is still pointing to the beginning of the last CP/M sector written to disk. Since CP/M 1.4 BDOS directory operations use as their sector buffer the 128 bytes of memory starting at the current DMA address, the 128 bytes of memory at the end of the saved area and the 128 bytes at the end of each 16k portion of a large saved area will have been overwritten after being saved. Since the image on disk will be correct, the bug will not be catastrophic unless you're unaware of it and you try to save something twice.

What will be catastrophic is any attempt to save an area larger that the TPA. For example,

SAVE 170 TMP.COM

will hang a 48k system. Since the manner in which the system will crash is unpredictable—a sector of the directory overwrites 128 bytes of the CP/M resident—be sure to experiment with disks you can afford to lose.

The undocumented CP/M 1.4 BDOS function 30 (1E hex) can be used to remove this bug so that SAVE will leave memory untouched. In a 48k Tarbell system, for example, make the following changes in CCP. Off the end of the CCP code, at location ACD0—or at 1150 in the CCP image in CPM.COM loaded under DDT—install this code:

```
ACD0 E5          PUSH H
ACD1 118000      LXI H,0080H
ACD4 0E1E        MVI C,1EH
ACD6 CD0500      CALL 0005
```

```
ACD9 110001          LXI D,0100H
ACDC E1              POP H
ACDD C3ABAA          JMP 0AAABH
ACE0 CDB3A5          CALL INIT
ACE3 C360AC          JMP DONE
```

and at AAA8—or at 0F28 under DDT—change 11 00 01 to C3 D0 AC and at AADD—or at 0F5D under DDT—change C3 60 AC to C3 E0 AC.

With this patch installed, SAVE will cause BDOS directory operations to use the sector buffer at 0080, and, then, after SAVE is complete, it will invoke a BDOS initialize function to restore normal directory processing. "Normal" means that BDOS will use your sector data buffer for directory operations. CBASIC, for example, extracts directory information from the sector buffer after a search for file function.

The CP/M 1.4 BDOS function 30 evidently was installed specifically to correct this problem, but the introduction of CP/M 2.2 negated the need.

BDOS 1.4 normally will use the current sector buffer—whatever you last set as DMA address with a BDOS function 26—whenever it has to read the directory. If this operation creates a problem, BDOS 1.4 function 30 can be used to give BDOS a separate sector buffer for its directory operations. For example, early in the program you can use the sequence

```
LXI   D,DOSBUF      ;Set BDOS buff
MVI   C,30
CALL  0005
```

to establish a separate 128-byte directory buffer at DOSBUF for use by BDOS. Then you can set your own data buffer location with the sequence

```
LXI   D,MYBUF
MVI   C,26
CALL  0005
```

Your own disk reads and writes will use MYBUF, but any directory operations performed by BDOS will use DOSBUF.

Without the BDOS function 30, there is only one current DMA address. Its value is whatever was last set with a BDOS function 26. We could call this address DMA26. BDOS function 30 of CP/M 1.4 provides an additional current DMA address whose current value is whatever was set by the last BDOS function 30. We could call this address DMA30. If no function 30 has been called, then DMA30 = DMA26. Whenever BDOS 1.4 performs directory operations, it uses a 128-byte buffer at DMA30. BDOS function 14, read sector, and BDOS function 15, write sector, always use DMA26. If no function 26 has been called, then DMA26 = 0080. Any program that uses BDOS function 30 should exit by jumping to 0000 to restore DMA30 = DMA26 = 0080.

The problem addressed by CP/M 1.4 BDOS function 30 is sidestepped entirely in CP/M 2.2 simply by requiring CBIOS to provide for BDOS a 128-byte buffer dedicated to directory operations. Under CP/M 2.2, the BDOS function number 30 has an entirely different definition, being used to set file attributes. Any CP/M 1.4 user program in which BDOS function 30 is used cannot be run under CP/M 2.2 until this function has been deleted. The CCP of CP/M 1.4 will, of course, never be used under CP/M 2.2, and thus the patch to SAVE has no downstream disadvantage.

Printer Spooling

The term *spooling*, as applied to printers, originally meant to intercept character output directed to the printer and direct it instead to a large first-in first-out (FIFO) buffer provided in some kind of fast storage such as core memory or disk—the purpose being, of course, to decouple fast programs from slow printers.

Implementations of this original approach to printer spooling are available in both hardware and software form. A spooling facility implemented in hardware is essentially a FIFO memory device designed for connection between the computer and the printer. A software implementation intercepts character output to the CP/M LIST device and buffers it through a FIFO memory provided on disk. These implementations speed up printer-directed output operations by accepting characters at high speed for subsequent lower rate output to the printer itself. If your program sends print-out information directly to the printer rather than writing this information to a disk file, its operation can be accelerated by either of these types of spoolers.

On the other hand, if your program writes all print-out information to text files on disk, it is already decoupled from the printer. Text files created can be copied to the printer later during what would otherwise be idle computer time. Since a CP/M system typically accumulates a great deal of idle time waiting for the next character to be typed at the console, a disk-to-printer file copy utility program that runs in the background during this idle time can significantly improve system productivity.

A disadvantage of intercepting printer output in the CBIOS LIST subroutine is that the LIST subroutine most likely will have been called from BDOS. We can intercept LIST characters with no trouble and stash them in a sector buffer, but what we cannot do is call BDOS to write this sector to disk. On entry, BDOS stores the contents of the machine's stack pointer register, and then, after the requested function has been processed, BDOS restores the stack pointer to the saved value just before using RET to return to the calling program. If we call BDOS from CBIOS while BDOS is processing a user function, such as LIST output, the user program's stack pointer will be lost. BDOS is "nonreentrant." A spooling utility set up to intercept LIST output in CBIOS must handle all its disk operations through CBIOS without help from BDOS. Such a spooler must duplicate BDOS code or require prior creation of a CP/M file to preallocate space within which it can operate in nonstandard fashion.

Your program can solve half the printer bottleneck problem simply by writing all print-out information to disk rather than sending it directly to the LIST device. The second half of the problem can then be solved by intercepting CONSOLE input operations "in front of" BDOS rather than LIST output operations in CBIOS "behind" BDOS. A disk-to-printer file copy utility program can be loaded into memory just below CCP, and the vector at 0005 can be set to point to the beginning of this program. The utility can then examine each BDOS function requested. Functions other than console input requests can be passed immediately to BDOS. When console input is requested, the utility calls CONST to determine if console input is available. If it is, the utility steps aside and allows the request to be processed immediately by BDOS. When no input is available from the console, the utility calls BDOS to read print file information from the disk and write the information to the printer.

Print file processing can be made fully automatic by arranging the spool utility to scan the file name table in the disk directory for files of type .OUT, for example. Under this arrangement, print file processing is similar to the output queue processing found on larger computer systems. A CBASIC program, for example, can create a list file with file type .PRN, close the file, and then rename it type.OUT, to drop it into the output queue. The spooling utility, running all the while in the background, will pick up the file and print it. After the file has been printed, the spooling utility will either rename the file to mark it "processed" or erase it to empty the queue.

Index